W9-CKD-494

CRACKING
THE ★ ★ ★ ★ ★ ★ ★ ★ ★
FEDERAL
★ ★ ★ ★ ★ JOB CODE

CRACKING
THE ★ ★ ★ ★ ★ ★ ★ ★ ★ ★ ★ ★
FEDERAL
★ ★ ★ ★ ★ ★ JOB CODE

TIPS FOR TODAY'S
FEDERAL JOB SEEKER

CORLISS JACKSON

 iUniverse®

SOMERSET COUNTY LIBRARY
BRIDGEWATER, N. J. 08807

CRACKING THE FEDERAL JOB CODE
TOP SECRET TIPS FOR TODAY'S FEDERAL JOB SEEKER

Copyright © 2015, 2016 Corliss Taylor Jackson.

All rights reserved. No part of this book may be used or reproduced by any means, graphic, electronic, or mechanical, including photocopying, recording, taping or by any information storage retrieval system without the written permission of the author except in the case of brief quotations embodied in critical articles and reviews.

iUniverse books may be ordered through booksellers or by contacting:

iUniverse
1663 Liberty Drive
Bloomington, IN 47403
www.iuniverse.com
1-800-Authors (1-800-288-4677)

Because of the dynamic nature of the Internet, any web addresses or links contained in this book may have changed since publication and may no longer be valid. The views expressed in this work are solely those of the author and do not necessarily reflect the views of the publisher, and the publisher hereby disclaims any responsibility for them.

Any people depicted in stock imagery provided by Thinkstock are models, and such images are being used for illustrative purposes only.
Certain stock imagery © Thinkstock.

ISBN: 978-1-4917-8698-7 (sc)
ISBN: 978-1-4917-8697-0 (e)

Library of Congress Control Number: 2016902081

Print information available on the last page.

iUniverse rev. date: 03/29/2016

I dedicate this book to my family, in particular my three great girls - Ciara, Alanah and Mariah - who will inherit this world and make it a much better place. Your growth provides a constant source of joy and pride.

Elephant shoes!

ACKNOWLEDGMENTS

To my Federal Job Results family: Brooke Vaughn, Marissa Schofield, and Rachel Hightower. Thank you for continually and selflessly supporting the clients we serve, many of whom now influence integral operations for the US federal government. You are amazing!

To my first federal manager, mentor for almost a decade, and the most gentle giant I know, Steve Benowitz, thank you for introducing me to the bizarre world of federal human resources. Interestingly enough, I am forever grateful!

To Amethyst Polk, whose writing style and discovery of interesting facts make this dry topic palpable to the most discriminating of palettes, you are truly a gifted writer!

To my illustrators, Leslie and Greg Coley and Morgan Ryan, thank you for working so tirelessly to provide visual attractiveness to this book!

To my predator editor extraordinaire, Dr. Cecelia Taylor (my mom), without whom this book would make no sense to anyone but me, thank you for being so generous with both your time and talent. I love you!

Lastly, to the US Office of Personnel Management, thank you for your role in deciphering the convoluted federal hiring process. Without your support and availability of information, this book would not be possible.

CONTENTS

INTRODUCTION

MEET THE AUTHOR
CORLISS JACKSON
Federal Job Results.com

Global Career Development Facilitator and Instructor
Certified Federal Job Search Coach
Certified Federal Job Search Specialist
Certified Federal Résumé Writer

I vividly remember submitting my first application for a federal job in the spring of 1997. It was a big year for the world; we lost Princess Diana and Mother Teresa in one weekend. O. J. Simpson was on trial, and twenty-one-year-old Tiger Woods won the Masters. Steve Jobs returned to run Apple Computers, and Microsoft was named the world's wealthiest company ($261 billion). The world was quickly changing, and so was my career.

Listening to a playlist of Lenny Kravitz and the Spice Girls, it took me two weeks to compose six essays describing my knowledge, skills, and abilities (KSAs) and another weekend to tweak my federal résumé to perfection. I don't mean to imply that I worked on my application nonstop twenty-four hours a day, but somewhere between the opening of *Titanic* and the release of the first Harry Potter book, I found myself writing and editing KSA essays into the wee hours of the morning. I felt great about my twenty-one-page application because I had worked so incredibly hard on it and because I truly felt that I was the perfect candidate for the federal position. That dream job was listed at the GS-13 level, but I refused to sell myself short. I figured that if the Pathfinder could land on Mars that year, then I could certainly land a federal job. Plus, I had earned my master's degree just two short years earlier while working full-time; wouldn't that gain me a little credit?

The hard work paid off! I got hired! Yes, even though I had absolutely no clue what I was doing or what the federal HR staff would be looking for in my application,

I got the job. Looking back on it now, when the HR specialist made me a federal job offer, I had no idea that I had overcome a monumental challenge. At age twenty-six, I had landed a GS-13 federal job at the US Department of Health and Human Services! Fortunately for me, it all worked in my favor. I'll call it luck coupled with many prayers!

I spent the next seven years working in various HR positions, which involved staffing, recruitment, and career development. I moved to the US Office of Personnel Management (OPM), and I led agency-wide and government-wide HR projects and programs. In my close to a decade of experience as an insider federal HR specialist, I learned much about the federal application process and its nuances. There are volumes upon volumes of information and regulations related to the complex federal hiring process and how to make hiring selections. (As I said above, with my inexperience at the time, I am frankly astonished that I got hired!)

After resigning my GS-15 position at OPM to care for my three girls, I was approached by several individuals who were seeking federal employment. They were experienced in their fields, and I knew they would make great public servants. The challenge they faced was navigating the complex, convoluted cobweb of the federal hiring process. I quickly became aware that there was not enough information available to federal job seekers, and the information that *was* shared was not easily understood—and none of it was from an insider's perspective.

My experience applying for several federal positions, coupled with the in-depth knowledge I gained while managing HR projects and programs in various organizations, has proven to be invaluable. Using this knowledge, I began to help individuals prepare federal application packages based on what I knew the federal HR professionals wanted and needed to see in federal applications. Word spread quickly that I was teaching those outside of the government how to navigate the federal application process—and they were getting it! I was invited to teach seminars at local one-stop career centers on how to crack the code of the federal hiring process. This led to invitations from military bases, colleges and universities, other local one-stop career centers, associations, and county venues. To date, I have delivered my message to thousands of individuals and organizations, resulting in an impressive track record of success. Individuals are getting interviews and job offers and making significant contributions to federal government operations.

This book is a compilation of the most important things you need to know about federal applications and hiring. It highlights what you need to know in order to create an extremely competitive federal application package. I have taken my signature seminar, which has helped thousands of federal job seekers, and created this book to guide you through the process of identifying the best jobs for your background, writing your federal résumé, and applying for federal jobs. Additionally,

I have included a section on federal interviewing because the process is incredibly competitive; if you interview, you want the job—not an invitation to go back to square one and start applying again.

My desire is that this information will be instrumental in your success as you apply for your dream positions within the federal government.

Good luck in cracking the code to your federal job search!

The Case for Federal Employment

You are not here merely to make a living. You are here in order to enable the world to live more amply, with greater vision, with a finer spirit of hope and achievement. You are here to enrich the world—and you impoverish yourself if you forget the errand.
　　　—Woodrow Wilson

There are a multitude of reasons why citizens seek careers in the federal government. Here are ten of the most popular motives behind the civil servant's journey:

Patriotism
The dedication of our federal workforce is vital to the challenges we face as a national and global community. A job in civil service allows you to make a positive difference in the lives of fellow Americans, directly affecting local, national, and global affairs.

Now Hiring!
An increase demand in health, science, and technology positions, coupled with the burgeoning rate of baby boomer retirement, is resulting in tens of thousands of available career opportunities.

Make a Difference

The US government is the biggest stage for addressing both national and international interests. Whether you are passionate about eradicating poverty, improving health care, preserving natural resources, or ensuring national security, there is a government program available just for you.

Travel the World

Nearly 85 percent of federal jobs are located outside of the DC metro area. Do you have the taste for travel? More than forty-four thousand federal employees serve their country abroad.

Diversity

The federal government has been a model for the private sector in advancing diversity in the workforce, and it actively encourages minorities and differently abled applicants to share their unique experiences, talents, education, and expertise in federal service. Additionally, the federal government does not have an age limitation; hiring managers are most interested in the skill sets of the applicant—not his or her age.

Something for Everyone

Federal jobs are not simply reserved for soldiers and politicians. The US government requires a plethora of skill sets from art history to zoology, social media design to robotics.

Unique Skills and Cutting-Edge Technology

The federal government has access to the latest in services and cutting-edge technology and can offer you a front-row seat to the latest innovations in information technology (IT), language immersion, professional development, and national security tools.

Tuition and Training

Some federal agencies may provide tuition assistance for those pursuing graduate-level degrees. Other programs also may help pay back up to $10,000 per year in student loans.

Work/Life Balance

Many agencies offer flexible work schedules (condensed workweeks, flexible start/end times, telework), gym memberships, on-site and/or reimbursement for child care, public transportation subsidies, dry-cleaning services, exercise classes and competitions, and a host of other employee-friendly programs and activities.

And drumroll, please …

Payday and Benefits!

Federal salaries are highly competitive and are coupled with world-class benefits, job stability, and opportunity for advancement. Benefits may include health care, life insurance, retirement, and Thrift Savings Plan (federal version of 401(k)). Civil servants may also enjoy on-site amenities such as day care, gym memberships, and transportation benefits.

MYTH BUSTING THE FEDERAL JOB SEARCH

Myth 1: The federal government isn't hiring.

Because of federal budget cuts, hiring freezes, and sequestration, federal hiring has changed. But here's an insider tip: the federal government is *always* hiring. Government positions that are labeled "mission critical" will always be filled—with or without a hiring freeze. Mission-critical roles are identified by the agency and may include a variety of positions. Keep in mind that somebody's got to do the work!

Myth 2: The federal government is never hiring anyone in my field.

There might not be a huge demand for underwater basket weavers in the current federal hiring climate, but we do see daily roles posted that are inclusive of fine art and multicultural outreach. If you feel that you are experiencing a drought in your field (especially if you are highly specialized), consider widening your search by category and job role. The "Class of 2016" hiring spree will be earmarked for a multitude of roles in health care, IT, cyber, acquisition and shipyard workforces, disability-evaluation workforces, sexual assault prevention, transition assistance, and more. Consider how your specific set of skills may be useful in one of these "in-demand" roles.

Myth 3: The federal government only hires veterans.

According to the US Office of Personnel Management—the authority that monitors federal hiring—67 percent of 2014 federal hires were nonveterans. That means that two out of every three employees hired were not veterans, and one out of three were veterans. If you are a veteran, thank you for your service to our country. The US government works to honor those who have served and sacrificed for our country. In regards to the hiring process—US military veterans earn a ten-point advantage on their hiring paperwork, which is known as *Veterans' Preference*. (To understand more about the federal initiatives that assist veterans in gaining federal employment, read chapter 11.)

Myth 4: The federal government won't hire me because I am too old.

This may be the biggest myth in the book. Baby boomers make up the vast majority of the federal workforce—a statistic that scares the government in preparation of an exodus of brilliant-brained retirees. In contrast, millennials (persons under age thirty) now make up less than 7 percent of the federal workforce (25 percent of the US workforce)—a number that is dropping drastically, as top tech-talent millennials become attracted to the corporate perks of companies such as Google, Uber, and Facebook. According to the Partnership for Public Service (PPS, one of our favorite workforce-statistic organizations), persons over the age of fifty make up 45 percent of the federal workforce and 19 percent of all federal new hires.

Myth 5: The federal government won't pay me what I'm worth.

Federal salaries are highly competitive. The US Office of Personnel Management conducts ongoing studies of rates of pay for various types of work in order to keep the pay rates competitive. This allows for comparable pay in the private and public sectors. In some cases, the federal government pays more than the private sector. Additionally, government employees living in certain metropolitan areas with higher costs of living will receive locality pay, which levels out the playing field.

Myth 6: The federal government won't hire me because I'm overqualified.

With the federal government, there is really no such thing as being overqualified. "This guy's got so much experience that we just can't hire him" is not something you will hear from the federal HR team. If you are lacking experience, you will hear about it in the form of a rejected application. However, you may find that you get to a federal interview and the hiring manager is a little bit apprehensive about hiring you because you have more experience than her staff and a higher level of experience than she brings to the table. To make the hiring manager less apprehensive, make sure you have a good reason for your interest in a lower-level position. A good example is if you are trying to get your foot in the door for stability or benefits.

THE GOVERNMENT OF THE UNITED STATES

The United States government holds several calendar dates near and dear to its heart: August 2, 1776, saw the signing of the Declaration of Independence, January 1, 1863, witnessed Abraham Lincoln's Emancipation Proclamation, and August 14, 1945, will forever be known as Victory Day over the Axis of Evil in World War II.

We can add another victory to our collective history: today is the day you (seriously) choose to start your federal job journey. Whether you are a butcher, a baker, a candlestick maker, an attorney, a teacher, or a soldier, there is a position in the US government where you can use your skills and experience.

Perhaps you want the opportunity to serve your country—or you might just have a secret skill that you can't wait to share with the world. You may crave the excitement of working with the latest and greatest state-of-the-art technology or networking with the most influential professionals on the planet. You could simply desire a solid career with job security, top-notch benefits, and a few fun weeks of paid vacation each year. Whatever the agenda and the objective you have for your endgame, this book is designed to help you attain your goal.

Navigating the federal job application universe can be a timely, tedious, and overwhelming journey. We often feel as if our hard work and preparation have floated into a big black bureaucratic hole. The long wait for application acknowledgment can leave us feeling weightless, seeking gravity in our government conquests. This book will provide you with an insider's look at how to write a federal résumé, find a perfect federal job match, qualify for a federal job, and ace a federal interview—all key factors for solving the mysteries within the federal job search process.

This "case file" contains fun facts, career clues, and helpful hints to help you crack the code to your very own federal career case. So gather up your handy magnifying glass, put on your sleuth cap, track down your notepad and invisible ink pen, and maybe even bring along a trusty sidekick because we are about to crack the code to your federal job search!

The following paragraphs are a quick look back at the extraordinary history of the United States (US) and the journey our founding fathers took from a ragtag bunch of British colonies to becoming a global superpower. (If you are a history buff, feel free to skip this quick review and move on to the next chapter.)

The US declared its independence from Great Britain on July 4, 1776, was recognized as a nation state on September 3, 1783, and embraced the Constitution of the United States on June 21, 1788. The price of freedom has brought the American people through the Revolutionary War, the Civil War, Spanish-American War, World War I, World War II, the Korean War, the Cold War, the Vietnam War, Desert Storm, and the Iraq and Afghanistan conflicts.

The US expanded from thirteen small colonies into fifty states, one federal district, and fourteen territories (five of which are populated). The federal government was meticulously designed into three branches—executive, legislative, and judicial—to maintain a balance of power. The legislative branch is made up of 100 senators and 435 congressmen and women. The US is considered a superpower and holds a permanent seat on the United Nations Security Council.

There are fifteen executive departments, each run by an appointed leader with the title of secretary (e.g., secretary of state). Each department has domain over specific agencies, programs, projects, budget, and staff as determined by the US Congress.

UNITED STATES EXECUTIVE BRANCH AGENCIES				
Department	Est.	Budget 2014	Employees	Website
State	1789	$49 billion	49,900	State.gov
Treasury	1789	$13.3 billion	115,897	Treasury.gov
Defense (War)	1789	$526.6 billion	3,230,000	Defense.gov
Interior	1849	$12 billion	71,436	DOI.gov
Agriculture	1862	$20.9 billion	105,778	USDA.gov
Justice	1870	$27.4 billion	113,543	Justice.gov
Commerce	1903	$8.2 billion	43,880	Commerce.gov
Labor	1913	$12 billion	17,477	DOL.gov
Veterans Affairs	1930	$63.2 billion	278,565	VA.gov
Health and Human Services	1953	$78.3 billion	76,341	HHS.gov
Housing and Urban Development	1965	$32.8 billion	10,600	HUD.gov
Transportation	1967	$17.8 billion	58,622	DOT.gov
Energy	1977	$25.6 billion	109,000	Energy.gov
Education	1979	$71.2 billion	5,000	ED.gov
Homeland Security	2002	$39.3 billion	240,000	DHS.gov

Works Cited: (Brown 2013), (Moore 2014)

US FUN FACT

In 1789, the US established its first three executive departments within weeks of each other: Department of State, Department of War, and Department of Treasury. The Department of War has since been renamed and restructured into the Department of Defense (1949).

Most US students grow up with a healthy dose of patriotism in elementary school: writing reports about their favorite states, playing the role of George Washington in their holiday "founding fathers" recital, or watching how a bill becomes a law on *Schoolhouse Rock*. Our classroom antics focused on the branches of government, but they didn't delve into federal departments, agencies, or subagencies. Here is the definitive list of all the federal entities that you may apply to in your government job search—without the anxiety of school picture day!

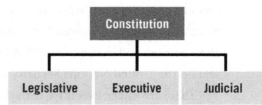

LEGISLATIVE BRANCH		
• US Congress		• Government Printing Office
• US Senate		• Library of Congress
• Architect of the Capital		• Congressional Budget Office
• US Botanical Garden		• Government Accountability Office

EXECUTIVE BRANCH	
• President, Vice President, Executive Office	• Office of Management and Budget
• White House Office	• Office of National Drug Control Policy
• Office of the Vice President	• Office of Policy Development
• Council of Economic Advisors	• Office of Science and Technology Policy
• Council of Environmental Quality	• Office of the US Trade Representative
• National Security Council	• Office of Administration

JUDICIAL	
• Supreme Court of the United States	• US Office of Appeals for Armed Forces
• United States Courts of Appeals	• United States Tax Court
• United States District Courts	• US Court of Appeals, Veterans Claims
• Territorial Courts	• Administrative Office, US Courts
• US Court of International Trade	• Federal Judicial Center
• US Court of Federal Claims	• United States Sentencing Commission

15 EXECUTIVE BRANCH DEPARTMENTS		
• Agriculture	• Health and Human Services	• Labor
• Commerce	• Homeland Security	• State
• Defense	• Housing and Urban Development	• Transportation
• Education	• Interior	• Treasury
• Energy	• Justice	• Veterans Affairs

42 EXECUTIVE OFFICE SUBAGENCIES	
• African Development Foundation	• Federal Election Commission
• Broadcasting Board of Governors	• General Services Administration
• Central Intelligence Agency	• Inter-American Foundation
• Commodity Futures Trading Commission	• Merit Systems Protection Board
• Corporation for National Community Service	• National Aeronautics and Space Admin.
• Defense Nuclear Facilities Safety Board	• National Archives and Records Admin.
• Environmental Protection Agency	• National Capital Planning Commission
• Equal Employment Opportunity Commission	• National Credit Union Administration
• Export-Import Bank of the United States	• National Foundation Arts and Humanities
• Farm Credit Administration	• National Labor Relations Board
• Federal Communications Commission	• National Mediation Board
• Federal Deposit Insurance Corporation	• National Railroad Passenger Corporation

• Federal Election Commission	• National Science Foundation
• Federal Housing Finance Board	• National Transportation Safety Board
• Federal Labor Relations Authority	• Nuclear Regulatory Commission
• Federal Maritime Commission	• Occupational Safety and Health Review
• Federal Mediation and Conciliation Service	• Director of National Intelligence
• Federal Mine Safety and Health Review	• Office of Government Ethics
• Federal Reserve Commission	• Office of Personnel Management
• Retirement Thrift Investment Board	• Office of Special Counsel
• Federal Trade Commission	• Overseas Private Investment Corporation
• Federal Deposit Insurance Corporation	

FEDERAL BUDGET (AND DEFICIT)

So far in this century, the US has overcome a major terrorist attack on US soil, two long-term occupations in Iraq and Afghanistan, and an economic recession starting in 2007, which left government coffers strained at best. What this means to the job seeker is that the federal government will be practicing budget discretion when bringing on new team members, and they will be investing in only the best candidates who can add the most value to the organization. Candidates with multiple skill sets will be in high demand.

2014 FUNDING: AGENCY-BY-AGENCY BREAKDOWN OF SPENDING BILL FEDERAL NEWS RADIO, 1500 AM			
Department	2014 Funding	Comparison	Highlights
Agriculture	$20.9 billion	+ $350 million above FY 2013	The Food Safety and Inspection Service will receive a $1 billion increase in funds, and the Farm Service Agency is slated to receive a boost of $1.5 billion.
Commerce	$8.2 billion	+ $113 million above FY 2013	$3 billion set aside for the US Patent and Trademark Office as well as $850 million to the National Institute of Standards and Technology and $5.3 billion to the National Oceanic and Atmospheric Administration.
Defense	$572 billion	(–) $32.7 billion below FY 2013	$486.9 billion in base funding plus $85.2 billion for overseas war expenditures. This bill provides $160 billion for operations and maintenance.
Education	$70.6 billion	(–) $739 million below FY 2013	There is a small boost to education grant spending.

2014 FUNDING: AGENCY-BY-AGENCY BREAKDOWN OF SPENDING BILL FEDERAL NEWS RADIO, 1500 AM			
Department	2014 Funding	Comparison	Highlights
Energy	$25.6 billion	+ $1.1 billion above FY 2013	$11.2 billion allocated to the National Nuclear Security Administration, $5.1 billion to science research, and $1.9 billion toward renewable energy programs.
Labor	$12.1 billion	(–) $449 million below FY 2013	Funding decrease for both the Employment Training Administration and Office of Job Corps, but adds funds to Veterans Employment and Training Services.
Health and Human Services	$78.3 billion	(+/–) Equal to FY 2013	$1.5 billion set aside to support online health insurance marketplaces and $26 million to convert to electronic health records. Mental health treatment programs will gain $130 million.
Homeland Security	$39.3 billion	(–) $336 million below FY 2013	An additional $10.6 billion has been allocated to Customs and Border Protection (CBP) to add 2,000 CBP officers.
Housing and Urban Development	$32.8 billion	(–) $687 million below FY 2013	The bill blocks allocated funds for "green" and "sustainable" community development programs.
Interior	$12 billion	+ 500 million	Geological Survey receives $1.2 billion, while energy-related programs will see $772 million and Wildland Fire Management earns $776.9 million.
Justice	$27.4 billion	+ $338 million above FY 2013	$395 million proposal toward programs to decrease gun violence, including $173 million to increase background checks.
State	$49 billion	(–) $4.3 billion below FY 2013	Embassy security received $5.4 billion, $25 million more than requested by the Obama administration. USAID receives a lowered $1.3 billion (budget cut).
Transportation	$17.8 billion	(–) 164 million below FY 2013	Discretionary funds plus $53.5 billion in nondiscretionary "obligation limitation."
Treasury	$13.3 billion	(–) 526 million below FY 2013	$92 million to address identity theft, refund fraud, and improve taxpayer services.
Veterans Affairs	$147.9 billion	+ 2.3 billion above FY 2013	$323 million set aside to bolster DOD electronic health records as well as $318 million to reduce a backlog of disability claims and $90 million to pay claims processors' overtime.
Medicare/Medicaid	$3.7 billion	(–) $195 million below FY 2013	$305 million will be used to process and pay benefits; however, additional funds may not be allocated toward the Affordable Care Act expenditures.

2014 FUNDING: AGENCY-BY-AGENCY BREAKDOWN OF SPENDING BILL FEDERAL NEWS RADIO, 1500 AM			
Department	2014 Funding	Comparison	Highlights
NASA	$17.6 billion	+ $120 million above FY 2013	$4.1 billion is provided for the Exploration mission, with an overall $781 million boost.
National Institutes of Health	$29.9 billion	(–) $714 million below FY 2013	A small drop from post-sequestration discretionary funds ($30.6 billion).
National Science Foundation	$7.2 billion	(–) $82 million below FY 2013	Budget levels have been restored with $288 million in funding, aimed to provide grant money to teachers and scientists.
Environmental Protection Agency	$8.2 billion	(–) $143 million below FY 2013	A "safety net" of $86 million has been set aside to stave off possible furloughs.
General Services Administration	$9.4 billion	+ $1.3 billion above FY 2013	$1.65 billion has been allocated for the construction and repair of federal buildings and courthouses from the Federal Buildings Fund ($9.4 billion).
Internal Revenue Services (IRS)	$11.3 billion	(–) $526 million below FY 2013	The Treasury Inspector General is to receive $156.4 million, while $92 million will be dedicated to stave off identity theft.

Works Cited: (Brown 2013), (Moore 2014)

MEET YOUR "HIRE" POWER

The US Office of Personnel Management (OPM) is dedicated to "recruiting, retaining, and honoring a world-class workforce for the American people." To many, OPM is known as the human resources (HR) arm of the federal government (and also the entity that closes Washington, DC, government offices during an emergency or inclement weather). To job seekers, OPM serves as the entity that directly or indirectly assesses federal résumés and qualifications for placement into federal positions. OPM takes its responsibility quite seriously; it is charged with recruiting and developing an all-inclusive workforce and building a global team rich in diverse ideas, backgrounds, cultures, interests, abilities, and perspectives. Individual agencies may have their own HR offices (or contracted staff), relying on OPM as a resource for guidance and support. Additionally, agencies can use OPM's services and expertise, such as background security clearances and training programs. For updates on HR policy and reform, go to the OPM website (OPM.gov).

As a federal job "investigator," you may consider OPM to be your secret laboratory—the place where all the application evidence is located, assessed, analyzed, and cross-examined for proof of hiring eligibility. Once you have cracked the code to your federal job search and taken the federal government employee oath of office, OPM will serve as one of your main personnel resources on federal benefits such as pay, leave, health care, retirement, and life insurance.

US FUN FACT

Prior to the invention of the Internet and the creation of the USAJOBS website, US citizens had to go to their local post offices to find a list of open federal government opportunities. Individual job posts were placed in large binders or tacked to bulletin boards for candidates to browse through at their leisure.

The Future of the Federal Workforce

My fellow Americans, ask not what your country can do for you, ask what you can do for your country.
—President John F. Kennedy

For more than twenty years during the Cold War, the US government enlisted civilian and military personnel as "psychic spies" who functioned as secret weapons for espionage (seriously, folks, we can't make this stuff up!). These "remote viewers," hired first by the US Pentagon, were able to infiltrate any target, elude elusive forms of security, and never risk a scratch. These parapsychology spies were selected for psychic ability, trained, and put to work against legitimate intelligence targets in real time. The program was so surprisingly effective that more than a dozen agencies adopted the same course of action, including the Central Intelligence Agency (CIA), Federal Bureau of Investigation (FBI), National Security Agency (NSA), Army, Navy, Secret Service, and US Special Forces command. For a little more psychic history (oxymoron?), check out articles at the Library of Congress by Jim Schnabel, such as "Remote Viewers: The Secret History of America's Psychic Spies." I'm not saying you need to be a psychic to obtain federal employment (although it certainly wouldn't hurt), but if you had access to futuristic information, would you use it?

The US government maintains a gargantuan amount of data on employment statistics to include growing fields of employment, forecasted workforce needs, and minority hiring trends. What is our favorite method of government job sleuthing? Cold. Hard. Facts. By assessing what's "trending" today, we can make our own predictions about tomorrow's workforce. Take that, psychic spies!

Federal New Hires—Class of 2014!

The following graphs and statistics are adopted from the Partnership for Public Service's "Fed Figures 2014," an annual report. These data include recent hiring information for full-time, nonseasonal, permanent civilian federal employees hired in fiscal year 2013 in executive branch agencies—excluding the US Postal Service. Please note that enlisted military personnel (air force, army, coast guard, navy, marines, and national guard) are excluded from these statistics. You can check out more helpful labor statistics at the US Department of Labor Bureau of Labor Statistics website.

It doesn't take a rocket scientist to know that the federal government likes to hire, well, rocket scientists. By far, the top fields of hire in the US government are those occupations falling under the categories of science, technology, engineering, mathematics, and medicine (STEM); 39 percent of all new employees hired in fiscal year 2013 were hired in these fields. This number has steadily increased by ten percentage points since 2009.

Do not stress if you are not a mathematician or an astrophysicist. There are plenty of support roles available to help you maximize your writing, communication, accounting, or culinary talents. Whatever your field, highlight the technology you used and the problems you solved. If you served as an administrative assistant, you may have worked with a customer database and managed schedules in Microsoft Outlook. If you were a financial analyst, you may have worked with Excel, Quicken, or SAP. Heck, even if you were the "go-to" person in the office every time the printer acted up, find a way to show off your technology skills. Troubleshooting comes in many forms.

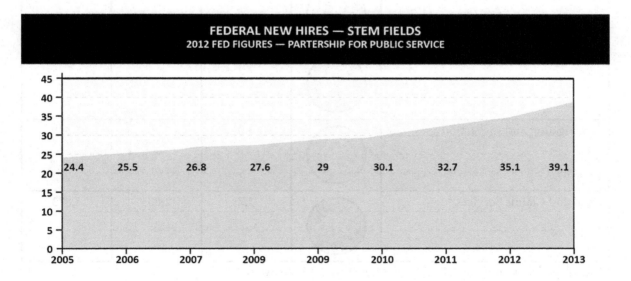

FEDERAL NEW HIRES — STEM FIELDS
2012 FED FIGURES — PARTERSHIP FOR PUBLIC SERVICE

FEDERAL HIRING BY OCCUPATION: 2012–2013				
		Percentage	2012	2013
Medical, Dental, and Public Health		26.9	20,646	19,493
Administration, Operations, and General Management		12.8	9,863	13,033
Other Occupations		6.5	4,993	5,227
Social Sciences and Psychology		5.6	4,281	4,420
Engineering and Architecture		4.7	3,633	4,504
Accounting and Budget		4.4	3,384	4,295
Information Technology		4.4	3,367	4,731
Business and Commerce		4.0	3,083	3,922
Investigation and Inspection		4.0	3,068	5,349
Legal and Claims Services		3.7	2,833	3,873

2012 Top Ten Occupational Groups for New Federal Employees
Source: Partnership for Public Service "Fed Figures"

OCCUPATIONAL GROUP	% OF TOTAL NEW EMPLOYEES	NEW EMPLOYEES	TOTAL EMPLOYEES
Legal and Kindred	4.3	3,873	99,220
Business and Industry	4.4	3,922	96,046
Accounting and Budget	4.8	4,295	116,516
Social Science, Psychology, and Welfare	4.9	4,420	84,158
Engineering and Architecture	5.0	4,504	128,623
Information Technology	5.3	4,731	80,492
Miscellaneous Occupations	5.8	5,227	82,369
Investigation	6.0	5,349	183,986
General Administrative, Clerical, and Office Services	14.5	13,033	296,224
Medical, Hospital, Dental, and Public Health	21.7	19,496	217,922

General Dwight D. Eisenhower, the heralded military commander of the Allied forces in WWII, warned many about the influence of the "military industrial complex" in his presidential farewell address. The general would not be surprised by today's US government new-hire statistics. With more than 79.8 percent of new employees being hired by defense and security-related agencies, 36 percent in the Department of Defense (DOD) alone (not including enlisted military personnel), Eisenhower's military industrial complex is alive and well.

2014 PERCENTAGE OF TOTAL NEW EMPLOYEES BY AGENCY 2014 FEDERAL FIGURES—PARTNERSHIP FOR PUBLIC SERVICE
Veterans Affairs 33.3
Army 12.5
Navy 9.7
Air Force 9.0
Justice 5.2
Homeland Security 5.1
Defense 5.0
Health and Human Services 4.7
Treasury 1.8
Agriculture 1.7
Other 12.0

They're not called the "Beltway Bandits" for nothing. No surprise here, the Washington, DC metro area (Maryland, DC, and Virginia) holds the lion's share of the federal jobs in the United States. However, there are plenty of government jobs to be had across all major population centers. The winners of the top federal job new-hire locations are:

10) New York

9) Pennsylvania

8) North Carolina

7) Georgia

6) Florida

5) Maryland

4) California

3) Washington, DC

2) Texas

1) Virginia

Agencies that have strong footholds in every state in the nation are the Department of Homeland Security, the Department of Transportation, the National Forest Service, and the Environmental Protection Agency. There are also federal thumbprints in Justice (federal circuit courts), Treasury, State, and Defense (military bases). You can also work, intern, or volunteer with your local member of Congress or state senator.

If you want to travel, you may want to check out federal job opportunities in other countries. The Department of State, US Agency for International Development (USAID), Department of Defense, and the Peace Corps may be great agencies with which to start your search. If you are looking for a position in a less populated area or if you are looking to work overseas, you may want to broaden your job search.

More than 50 percent of federal new hires in 2013 were under the age of forty, which simply means that the other new hires were over the age of forty. Federal hiring managers do not base their hiring decision upon how many followers you have on Twitter or how snazzy you look in your LinkedIn profile picture. For this reason, the federal government is an excellent place for mature professionals—and even senior citizens—to show off their skills. (And do we really want twenty-year-olds running the government?)

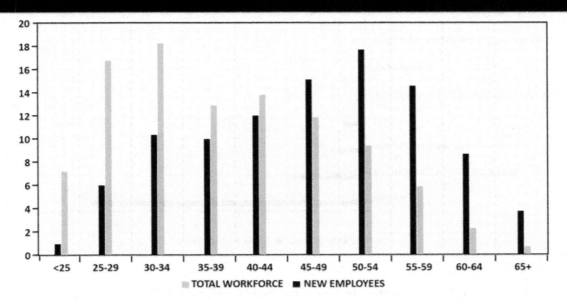

RECENT HIRING AND SEPARATION TRENDS
2012 FED FIGURES — PARTERSHIP FOR PUBLIC SERVICE

TOTAL WORKFORCE ■ NEW EMPLOYEES

There's no way around it—the federal workforce is aging. Various statistics have stated that nearly 40 percent of civil servants are eligible for retirement, meaning that they have either completed thirty years in the federal government or they have reached the age at which they can collect Social Security and/or retirement benefits. Why are they not retiring? There are a multitude of reasons why people aren't yet trading in their cubicles for condos on the beach. Some lost out in the recent market crashes and have been waiting to rebuild their retirement funds. Some workers are paying off their children's college or wedding debts or simply saving for a vacation home or a pool (you do not have to feel sorry for these people). Others simply don't want to leave their meaningful job (and paychecks).

The 2014 numbers are in, and this one may come as a bit of a shocker. The "Class of 2014" is slightly less racially diverse than the total federal workforce. Studies show that 32 percent of federal new hires in 2014 could be classified in a minority racial group, which is almost three percentage points less than the 35 percent of minority new hires in 2013. Despite the small decrease in minority hiring, the US population is still blossoming with an increase in minority growth. More Hispanic and Latino students are graduating from colleges and graduate schools. Many black and African American professionals are charting new career paths in cyber security and information technology (IT). Minorities have moved up the ranks within the US government into more senior and supervisory level positions. Outside of the federal workforce, minorities are breaking records in new fields throughout the private and nonprofit sectors, and many have opted to form their own businesses.

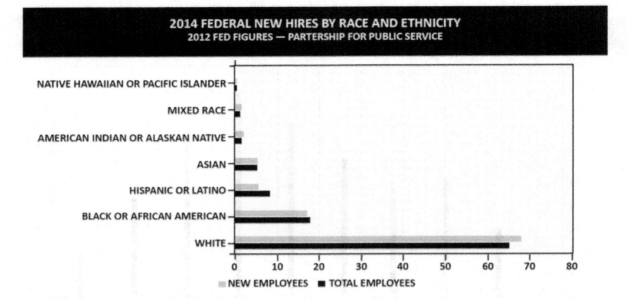

2014 FEDERAL NEW HIRES BY RACE AND ETHNICITY
2012 FED FIGURES — PARTERSHIP FOR PUBLIC SERVICE

Women may be from Venus, and men may be from Mars, but they both seem to be getting along quite well in the federal government. Women make up 42.6 percent of the federal workforce, moving up .1 percent in the "new hires" category from 2012 to 2013.

The vast majority of federal job postings will be categorized within the fifteen level, government-wide pay and classification system known as the General Service (GS) schedule, which is divided into grade and step, which equates to a dollar amount. Some agencies have adopted other pay scales (or pay ranges called "pay bands"), but the basic premise remains the same as the GS schedule. Federal salaries are competitive and can outshine the salaries of the private sector in many fields. In addition to their base pay, civil servants may enjoy additional income based on duty station, cost of living, and type of work performed. Federal positions can pay from GS-1 Step 1 to GS-15 Step 10. When you first enter into federal employment, the agency will generally offer you the lowest step of the grade, but you can negotiate salary (up to the Step 10 of the same grade) upon first entering federal service (see chapter 3 for negotiating salary).

					SALARY TABLE 2016-GS					
			INCORPORATING THE 1% GENERAL SCHEDULE INCREASE EFFECTIVE JANUARY 2016								
					Annual Rates by Grade and Step					
Grade	Step 1	Step 2	Step 3	Step 4	Step 5	Step 6	Step 7	Step 8	Step 9	Step 10	WITHIN GRADE AMOUNTS
1	$ 18,343	$ 18,956	$ 19,566	$ 20,173	$ 20,783	$ 21,140	$ 21,743	$ 22,351	$ 22,375	$ 22,941	VARIES
2	20,623	21,114	21,797	22,375	22,629	23,295	23,961	24,627	25,293	25,959	VARIES
3	22,502	23,252	24,002	24,752	25,502	26,252	27,002	27,752	28,502	29,252	750
4	25,261	26,103	26,945	27,787	28,629	29,471	30,313	31,155	31,997	32,839	842
5	28,262	29,204	30,146	31,088	32,030	32,972	33,914	34,856	35,798	36,740	942
6	31,504	32,554	33,604	34,654	35,704	36,754	37,804	38,854	39,904	40,954	1,050
7	35,009	36,176	37,343	38,510	39,677	40,844	42,011	43,178	44,345	45,512	1,167
8	38,771	40,063	41,355	42,647	43,939	45,231	46,523	47,815	49,107	50,399	1,292
9	42,823	44,250	45,677	47,104	48,531	49,958	51,385	52,812	54,239	55,666	1,427
10	47,158	48,730	50,302	51,874	53,446	55,018	56,590	58,162	59,734	61,306	1,572
11	51,811	53,538	55,265	56,992	58,719	60,446	62,173	63,900	65,627	67,354	1,727
12	62,101	64,171	66,241	68,311	70,381	72,451	74,521	76,591	78,661	80,731	2,070
13	73,846	76,308	78,770	81,232	83,694	86,156	88,618	91,080	93,542	96,004	2,462
14	87,263	90,172	93,081	95,990	98,899	101,808	104,717	107,626	110,535	113,444	2,909
15	102,646	106,068	109,490	112,912	116,334	119,756	123,178	126,600	130,022	133,444	3,422

Within-grade increases (WGIs) or step increases are periodic increases in a GS employee's rate of basic pay from one step of the grade of his or her position to the next higher step of that grade. The required waiting periods are established by law for advancement to the next higher step and are as follows:

Advancement From	Requires
Step 1 to Step 2	52 weeks of creditable service in Step 1
Step 2 to Step 3	52 weeks of creditable service in Step 2
Step 3 to Step 4	52 weeks of creditable service in Step 3
Step 4 to Step 5	104 weeks of creditable service in Step 4
Step 5 to Step 6	104 weeks of creditable service in Step 5
Step 6 to Step 7	104 weeks of creditable service in Step 6
Step 7 to Step 8	156 weeks of creditable service in Step 7
Step 8 to Step 9	156 weeks of creditable service in Step 8
Step 9 to Step 10	156 weeks of creditable service in Step 9

Of all of the employees hired by the US government in 2013, 38,717 or 50.7 percent have earned at least a four-year college degree. This is 1.6 percent increase from 2012 and is pretty significant considering that this increase happened in less than twelve months. Keep in mind that there are many jobs in the federal government that require a degree and many others that do not. You may see a high school graduate managing a government-wide program at a GS-15 level in the government. Not to be ignored, certifications are vital in today's federal workforce. Certifications in project management (PMP), ITIL, SAP, JAVA, or Security + can give a great boost to your experience. If your dream job requires a certification, earn it. If you simply need to brush up on some skills, try learning new skills on the Internet. The government will give you credit for your skills, regardless of how you gained them, as long as they are documented on your federal résumé.

RECENT HIRING AND SEPARATION TRENDS
2014 FED FIGURES — PARTERSHIP FOR PUBLIC SERVICE
(IN THOUSANDS)

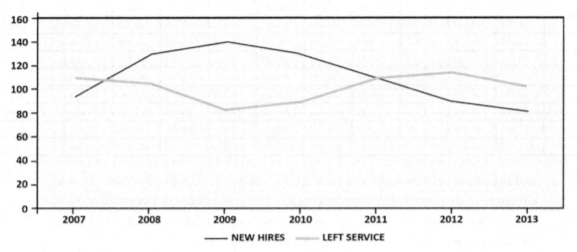

Veteran hiring has consistently risen since 2008, which is a direct correlation with the drawdown efforts from the Iraq and Afghanistan conflicts. The military has received many large-scale budget cuts, which has led to many of the men and women of our armed forces accepting early retirement packages. This means that a steady influx of veterans is joining the federal workforce for the next four to ten years. As the soldiers, sailors, and marines who enlisted in response to the September 11 terrorist attacks begin to wrap up their military service, they are forging new paths in their civilian lives. Many are cashing in their hard-earned education credits, and others are rejoining the private, nonprofit, or government sectors.

If you are not a veteran, do not be alarmed! These statistics may be causing you concern, not because you aren't thrilled to see the government taking care of those who have served our country, but because you feel the cards are a bit stacked against you right now. Be not dismayed! The government still seeks the most qualified applicant, and 68 percent of the federal workforce consists of fantastic individuals like you without a military background.

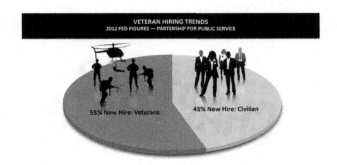

The Federal Job Road Map

I don't know anything that builds the will to
win better than competitive sports.
—Richard M. Nixon

Federal jobs are competitive. Researching government jobs that fit your skill set,
writing a star federal résumé, and not giving up are key factors to making it into the
big leagues.

It takes a lifetime of preparation and determination for a football player to make
it into the National Football League (NFL). Only the crème de la crème are invited to
participate. If one can physically make it through boot camp, he must wait for seven
draft stages to determine his final fate. Thirty-two teams will buy, sell, or trade to
acquire their favorite players—fifty-three to a team.

Qualifying for a federal job can be really tough, but it is not impossible for those
who put the work into it. Much like the NFL selection process, your résumé will be
assessed from every angle and compared to the many other applicants competing for
the same position. If your application makes it through the qualifying rounds, it will
be up to a select panel of hiring officials to cherry-pick the final handful of candidates
to interview. After the top tier is cross-examined, the panel will make its final decision
on which candidate(s) will be selected for the position(s).

US FUN FACT

If the US government had its own fantasy football league, it would include five US presidents who played college football: Dwight Eisenhower (West Point), Gerald Ford (Michigan, team MVP), John F. Kennedy (Harvard), Richard Nixon (Whittier College), and Ronald Reagan (Eureka College).

The federal application and hiring process can be daunting. It is a long process and will take commitment and persistence on your part. Some agencies have been able to adhere to the eighty-day hiring model put forth by OPM. Generally, we have found that it can take anywhere from three to eighteen months to land a federal position. It will depend on a multitude of variables:

- how many agencies are looking for candidates with your qualifications
- how many applications you submit
- which locations you are interested in searching
- how specialized your skill set is—the more specialized you are, the quicker your trek will be (but there may be fewer job openings)
- how generalized your skill set is (the more generalized you are, the more job openings you will find to be available), however, there will more competition
- how thorough and detailed your federal résumé is
- agency funding and congressional budget issues
- how well you interview

Unfortunately, your favorite aunt, rich uncle, best friend, or beloved neighbor will not be able to snag you a job in the federal government. This is because the federal hiring process has been rewired to create a level playing field for applicants. Prior to 1883, all federal hiring was left to the "spoils system," which meant that the president, political party, or administration holding power at the time held full authority over the hiring and firing of federal workers.

The former Civil Service Commission (now OPM), which was established by the dynamic President Theodore "Teddy" Roosevelt, built a more impartial, professional, and unbiased hiring approach. This new initiative took power away from political favors, and constructed a new hiring system based on merit and skill, and based on the idea that the job should go to the citizen who could best execute the demands of the position. Today's job seeker is the direct beneficiary of this hiring policy. Of course, we've all heard of cases in which an applicant knows someone on the inside and ends up getting the job. It is not without competition. The individual has to first get through the HR qualification screening process and then the hiring panel; both feats are easier said than done.

The US Department of Agriculture (USDA) is arguably one of the most efficient organizations when it comes to maximizing growth, quantity, quality, and sustainability. The USDA staff work around the clock—and around the world—to ensure that we enjoy the safest and healthiest fruits, vegetables, grains, and meat products at our dinner tables.

In one of USDA's latest studies, the National Institute of Food and Agriculture was able to partner with Purdue University scientists from Wisconsin, Michigan, and New Jersey through a grant program testing the effects of light-emitting diodes (LED) illumination on plants in greenhouses. Researchers designed LEDs to produce the exact quality of light needed to help plants thrive at their pinnacle for photosynthesis. Results revealed a 75 percent reduction in electricity used as compared to high-pressure sodium lamps—the current industry standard.

US FUN FACT

America is home to more than 4,200 acres of greenhouses. If LED systems were introduced into each greenhouse, energy use would be reduced by 3.5 billion kilowatt hours, reducing carbon dioxide emissions by almost three million tons per year.

Your hiring team is similar to a team of gleaming-eyed USDA scientists. Through a wide range of steps, tests, and assessments, they are trying to determine the smartest, safest, and most efficient results for their federal workforce needs.

Far too many federal job applicants believe that once they hit the "submit" button, their federal application enters a black hole. This should not be the case. If applicants can understand that there is a formula for which the HR team is looking, it really can help produce a winning federal application. But understanding that formula is key to cracking the code to your federal job search.

For most vacancy announcements, the applicant will submit an online application. There are several systems that exist for this purpose, but for each vacancy announcement, there are specific instructions that must be followed, which can be found in the vacancy announcement. The most commonly used application system is the USAJOBS website.

Once the vacancy announcement has closed or when the minimum number of applications has been received (as stated in the vacancy announcement), the federal HR team will rate and rank the applications. The HR team rates applicants based on a document they call a *crediting plan*. The crediting plan provides them with the information they need—and they compare the crediting plan with your résumé. The more information they see on your résumé, the more credit you get in the process. Details such as how work was accomplished, what skills were utilized, and in what processes you engaged are extremely important. They are primarily looking for three components:

THE SELF-ASSESSMENT QUESTIONNAIRE

Most vacancy announcements will have an assessment questionnaire, which consists of about ten to a hundred multiple-choice questions about the applicant's skills as related to the specific job duties and qualifications for the targeted job. This part of the process is extremely important because the final score on this assessment will determine whether or not the application will move forward in the hiring process. It is a system—not a human being—that determines whether or not the applicant will move forward in the process. Some applicants will move forward, and the rest will be filtered out and will not move forward in the process.

Don't be modest! If you are reading this book, we assume that you have the utmost character and serve as a role model for wise counsel, superb intellect, and exceptional leadership. The words *braggart, arrogant,* or *supercilious* have never been used to describe you—and never will. However, now is the time to step up your game! For this questionnaire, you will need to brag, boast, sell, market, and claim as much professional swagger as you can muster. You need to answer each question with the response that best describes your highest level of knowledge, skill, and ability on the topic. We are not telling you to be arrogant or untruthful, but we are asking you to put on your best game face and give yourself full credit for the many years of hard work, education, training, volunteer work, and dedication you have invested into your career. This is your chance to let your future employer know your full, all-inclusive, unhindered, and unlimited potential.

In most cases, the system will assign a value to each response, generally A through E. Your total score from this questionnaire will determine if you will move forward in the federal hiring process. You will need to answer each question at the highest level of knowledge, skill, and ability possible as it applies to your life and career. Seize this opportunity to brag, boast, sell, and market your greatest professional assets. In many cases, the highest-ranking answer will be classified as E, but just like all multiple-choice tests, make sure to fully read each question and respective answer options prior to answering each selection (just in case). Test makers always want to keep test takers on their toes.

Problem Solving: Identifies and analyzes problems, uses sound reasoning to arrive at conclusions, and finds alternative solutions to complex problems.	
A	I have not had education, training, or experience in performing this task.
B	I have had education or training in performing the task but have not yet performed it on the job.
C	I have performed this task on the job. My work on this task was monitored closely by a supervisor or senior employee to ensure compliance with proper procedures.
D	I have performed this task as a regular part of a job. I have performed it independently and normally without review by a supervisor or senior employee.
E	I am normally the person who is consulted by other workers to assist them in doing this task because of my expertise.

CAREER CLUE

Be very generous in your self-assessment responses. We call it "marketing yourself." Do not be dishonest—but give yourself full credit for all work, training, education, skills, and volunteer work you have mastered in your career. Paid and unpaid experience counts. Do not be modest!

Sell yourself! Your career is not a deserted island consisting of only your previous job. Do not forget to consider all positions, part-time or temporary assignments, internships, projects, research, published work, awards, education, training, and volunteer opportunities you have experienced when answering the self-assessment questions. You may not have held the title of "supervisor" on your last contract as a cybersecurity analyst, but you may have supervised a software transition project, led a focus group, trained twelve coworkers on database input, or presented your research findings to management. All of these activities can help to classify you as a desirable professional with exemplary supervisory skills—regardless of the formal title. Furthermore, the skills you have gained taking night school, volunteering for a religious organization, organizing a charity golf tournament, or coaching your child's softball or soccer team can add value to your total candidate package. Do not discount your extracurricular interests, community involvement, or leadership in professional organizations. Your self-assessment responses should reflect all sparkling facets of your personal and professional life.

KEY WORDS

Once the computer system has passed you through to the next step in the process, the second thing for which the HR team is looking is key words. They will scan with human eyeballs (not using a system or technology) the application and look subjectively for the applicant to have included the desired key words.

CAREER CLUE

Copy and paste the contents of the federal vacancy "duties" and "qualifications and evaluations" section into TagCrowd.com. Select "Visualize!" This website will morph the paragraphs into bolder, bigger words that highlight the most frequently used terms and phrases in your target job description. Then, incorporate them into your federal résumé.

FEDERAL RÉSUMÉ

Once the HR team has decided that the applicant has enough of the "right" key words, the next step is that they will want to read the résumé (again with human eyeballs). They are not looking for a private- or corporate-sector résumé; a federal résumé is much different. Did you know there was a difference between private-sector and corporate-sector résumés and a federal résumé? Now you do!

Next, the HR team will decide which applicants move forward. Generally there are three tiers. The bottom tier leaves the applicant behind (not eligible to move forward). The second tier is very common; "eligible—not referred" means the applicant is applying to the right types of jobs, but the résumé doesn't include enough information to support moving forward. (Think of going in the right direction but traveling in a Dodge Gremlin or Ford Pinto). The result is that the applicant will not move forward. Applicants need to be in the top tier in order to move forward to the hiring manager (which is called a "referral" or "making the certificate of eligible applicants list"). At this point, HR has completed their assessment.

From these lists of eligible applicants, the hiring manager will now decide who (if anyone) to contact for an interview. The federal interview is extremely competitive, and you need to be fully prepared for it (see chapter 9).

Once the interview process is complete, the hiring manager will let the HR team know the top candidate for the position. The HR team will continue with the remainder of the hiring process.

HR will extend an offer of employment that is contingent on a successful background investigation by the agency's security office (see chapter 15).

When you first enter into federal employment, the agency will most likely offer you the lowest step of the grade (step 1), but you can negotiate pay (up to the step 10 of the same grade) upon first entering federal service. You can also negotiate your accrued leave category. Generally, when you first start, you will accrue four hours of leave per pay period (about two weeks). You can negotiate to receive up to eight hours of accrued leave per pay period (about a month) when you first start. This is the only time you can negotiate! If you wish to negotiate your starting salary, we recommend sending a justification e-mail to the HR point of contact along with at least two recent pay stubs showing a salary higher than the step 1 of the grade to which you are applying. Below is an example of a typical negotiation letter. Of course, it will need to be tailored to your situation.

Sample Salary Negotiation Justification E-mail

Dear Ms. Hines:

Thank you for quickly assembling a tentative offer for the program analyst position. I'd like to negotiate an increased step-level negotiation based on my experience and the unique skills required by the position.

Based on my previous position at the White House, I developed an extensive network of connections to support my position as an airlift coordinator for the president, vice president, first family, as well as cabinet-level, congressional delegations, and senior government officials. I was an expert in interpreting policy guidance, DOD regulations, and air-mobility procedures, and I rewrote operational policy for the current administration to clearly define the use of military aircraft on White House support requests that will be used across all federal agencies and branches of government. My extensive record of success also extends to supporting more than three thousand airlift missions deployed globally with 100 percent success for the White House through my intimate knowledge and ability to locate and utilize worldwide assets.

My performance in a high-profile environment, my specialized skill set, and my previous salary of $150,000 (attached recent Leave and Earnings Statement) make me a strong candidate for starting at a G-15 step 8 with locality pay.

Additionally, as a result of twenty-two years of military service, I would like to request leave at a rate of eight (8) hours per pay period, which would equate with my last position.

Thank you for your consideration of my request. If you have any questions, I will reply to them as soon as possible.

Sincerely,
Sherlock Holmes

Pieces to the Puzzle: Clues from an Insider

If you're walking down the right path and you're willing
to keep walking, eventually you'll make progress.
— Barack Obama

A sharp detective tracks an unsolved case from beginning to end by creating a visible storyboard—a life-sized chalkboard or bulletin board full of pictures and documents connecting characters, clues, evidence, and events in sequential order. Before we get into the nitty-gritty of quirky qualifications or remarkable résumés, let's take a moment to assess some pieces of the puzzle.

If you are like us, you spend a little time each day wondering why we are not yet driving flying vehicles, riding floating skateboards, or having our dishes washed by robots. What happened to the snazzy future devices we were promised in cartoons as children? For the US government, those days are being lived out right now. It may surprise some that the US Department of Transportation has in fact been fine-tuning vehicle-to-vehicle (V2V) communications for safety since 2002. This technology accelerates a dynamic wireless exchange of data between nearby vehicles, offering the opportunity for important safety improvements. Vehicle-based data comparing the position, speed, and location of other automobiles allows vehicles to recognize hazards and potential threats with 360-degree awareness, ultimately reducing human error and nearly eliminating life-threatening auto accidents.

Source: US Department of Transportation

If you knew that a little preparation and research would help you create a whole new job market and save lives, would you do it? Any engineer, scientist, or detective would tell you that assessing facts, gathering evidence, and collaborating with your team prior to fieldwork or conclusions is pivotal in building a hospital, curing a disease, or solving a crime. This section highlights several clues, insider information, and research and development, to help you land your federal dream job. And, yes! You may work on this from your hovercraft.

QUALIFYING FOR A FEDERAL JOB

Direct Work Experience

There are myriad ways to present your knowledge, skills, and abilities on your federal résumé. However, there are two main avenues you may take to reach your final federal job destination: direct work experience and/or transferable skills. If you currently hold or held in the past decade a position that is very similar to that which you are applying and you have performed that work for a minimum of twelve months, then you may apply for that federal job by using your direct work experience. The twelve months does not need to be consecutive (two projects worked on for six months each separated by a year will count). The twelve months does need to be at least forty hours per week (full-time) or the equivalent (twenty-four months working at twenty hours per week would equate to twelve months).

Transferable Skills

If you have acquired a set of skills (in a paid or unpaid environment) that align with the federal government's needs and have performed that work for a minimum of twelve consecutive or nonconsecutive months, then you may apply for that federal job by using your transferable skills or transferable work experience. If you are trying to change careers, focus on your transferable skills and leverage those to get your foot in the door. Then, after your probationary period has been fulfilled, target the job you really want by using access to training, networking, and volunteer opportunities that may help facilitate a career change.

CAREER CLUE

If you can position yourself to meet your target organization's needs, they will hire you. The government may not be in need of jewelry store managers, but a program manager with skills in finance, procurement, human resources, operations, contracting, and inventory control might be exactly what is needed. Now is the time to highlight what is special about you as it relates to your target organization's needs.

TARGETING THE RIGHT FEDERAL JOB

In the federal government, similar job duties and responsibilities are grouped together in categories known as *job series*. Over 400 job series exist within the federal government. Understanding which job series best fits your personal experience is vitally important to your federal job search. Regardless of the agency to which you apply or the location of the position, the duties performed and skills required for a job series are similar. In USAJOBS, on the overview tab, there is a section titled "Series and Grade." Job series is the four-digit number listed between the pay scale ("GS") and the grade ("12"). Within the federal government—regardless of department, agency, or country in which the work is performed—jobs with similar duties and similar required skill sets will be placed in the same job series for classification purposes. One of the many searches that can be initiated on the USAJOBS website is a job series search (see chapter 14). Most applicants will discover that they will qualify for several (probably one to four) job series. By focusing on the target, applicants should be able to create a sharper résumé and focus time and energy on only those positions for which one is qualified.

Each job series falls under an umbrella category known as an *occupational group*. Each occupational group encompasses multiple job series numbers. The first two digits of the job series number ("03" in the above example) will help you identify the overarching occupational group to which the job series belongs. If you have supported or managed a program, project, or process (for at least twelve months), you should look at the 0300 occupational group (see chapter 14). If you have subject matter expertise in a particular field (for at least twelve months), you may find that you should also look at a second and possibly third (or fourth) occupational group. For example, if you have expertise in information technology (IT), you should look at the 2200 occupational group. One of the many searches that can be initiated on USAJOBS website is an occupational group search (see chapter 14). For more information on occupational groups and job series, visit the OPM website and search for the *Handbook of Occupational Groups and Families.*

23 WHITE-COLLAR OCCUPATIONAL GROUPS	
0000	Miscellaneous Occupations
0100	Social Science, Psychology, and Welfare
0200	Human Resources Management
0300	General Administrative and Clerical
0400	Natural Resources Management and Biological Sciences
0500	Accounting and Budget
0600	Medical, Hospital, Dental, and Public Health
0700	Veterinary Medical Science
0800	Engineering and Architecture
0900	Legal and Kindred
1000	Information and Arts
1100	Business and Industry
1200	Copyright, Patent, and Trademark
1300	Physical Sciences
1400	Library Sciences

1500	Mathematical Sciences
1600	Equipment, Facilities, and Services
1700	Education Group
1800	Inspection, Investigation, Enforcement, and Compliance
1900	Quality Assurance, Inspection, and Grading
2000	Supply Group
2100	Transportation
2200	Information Technology

Dig Deeper

From the USAJOBS main menu, you can do a search. To look more closely at a particular announcement, select the duties tab to see a list of bullets or paragraphs describing the job requirements (usually there are about six to eight). Pay particular attention to the verbs from each requirement: analyze, report, track, etc. These verbs are the core skills that the HR staff is looking to see on your résumé, and they need to see that you have performed about 80 percent of the six to eight requirements. Additionally, know that the order in which the requirements are listed is important— they are listed in order of priority, and they are weighted—with the requirement at the top of the list being weighted more heavily in the rating process than that at the bottom of the list. If you find that you have performed these core skills (for at least twelve months—consecutive or nonconsecutive), jot down the job series and occupational group numbers, and continue searching for other similar career opportunities. You should be able to identify a pattern in which several job series (probably up to three or four) and one to three occupational groups seem to be a good fit for you.

CAREER CLUE

Adopt the "80 Percent Rule." There are thousands of jobs floating around on the USAJOBS website waiting to be applied to by just the right candidate. How do you know if you are the ideal candidate? A good rule of thumb is to read the full vacancy announcement and then ask yourself if you have performed 80 percent of the duties for at least twelve months.

DUTIES: Back to top

This Program Analyst position is located in the Visible Intermodal Prevention and Response (VIPR) Program / Joint Coordination Center (JCC), Field Operations Division (FLD), within the Office of Law Enforcement/Federal Air Marshal Service (OLE/FAMS), Transportation Security Administration (TSA), Department of Homeland Security (DHS). If selected for this position, you will serve as a Program Analyst for the VIPR/JCC Program as the administrative interface providing overall operational support on a wide range of duties. Duties include but are not limited to:

- Providing information to management and employees to support decision-making regarding personnel policies, procedures, and action processing.
- Researching and preparing initial analyses of relevant qualitative and quantitative information to support objectives.
- Contributing to the development of findings and recommendations for improving the security and efficiency of TSA operations and programs.
- Responding to inquiries from internal and external groups and preparing information for action; executing special projects on critical initiatives.
- Performing financial and administrative reviews to ensure overall compliance with program requirements concerning financial and resource allocations, expenditures, and reports; compiling and summarizing financial and resource information and preparing a variety of reports; reporting results of projects, both orally and in writing, to program managers.
- Establishing and maintaining liaison with a variety of entities including, but not limited to, TSA Headquarters, OLE/FAMS FLD, Freedom Center, and Transportation Security Operations Center (TSOC).

The major duties described above reflect the full performance level of this position. Typically, the lower Pay Band (G Pay Band) perform the same duties but will receive more guidance and training; and projects or work assignments may be less complex.

Your central goal may be to achieve a certain rank in the federal government—one characterized by a high salary or level of responsibility. The federal HR team will use your federal résumé to determine if you are highly qualified for a specific career and GS level. Your résumé will be assessed for proof of knowledge, skill, ability, and leadership responsibilities. If you do not have any idea which grade level you qualify for, use your current salary as a baseline. You may apply to jobs at a higher or lower salary and may easily qualify since the decision will be based on your résumé. The federal government will not state that you are overqualified for a position, but a hiring manager interviewing you may get a bit intimidated regarding the experience or degree you would bring to the job if it makes him or her feel inferior. Additionally, for most applications, education will get you only so far. Education plus experience is the best-case scenario, but work experience alone can trump education. For more information on GS level of pay and responsibility, visit the OPM website.

In the past, vacancies with short time periods between the job opening and closing dates indicated that the agency probably had someone who was qualified applying for the job. It was advertised, but because there was a qualified applicant, the agency did not need an excessive number of applications. Presently, many agencies have the same short windows because they are seeking to limit the number of applications received. For example, the navy's standard window for a vacancy announcement to be open is four days.

KSA is the acronym for knowledge, skill, and ability statement. A KSA is a short statement that the federal government uses in vacancy announcements, and as the applicant, it is your job to prove. One of the most common KSAs, for example, is the "ability to communicate orally and in writing." Historically, federal job applicants documented their KSAs in the form of written essays (sometimes averaging two pages in length) with three to eight KSAs per vacancy announcement. In 2010, federal government hiring reform was passed, which eliminated the written essay requirement for 96 percent of the agencies. Quite frankly, the HR team did not wish to read multiple essays any more than applicants wanted to write them! While written KSAs may not be required during the initial application process, some agencies may require them later in the hiring process. Some agencies require written assessments (tests). Regardless, it is extremely important to make sure the KSAs are addressed in your federal résumé.

KSAs tell the hiring team what knowledge, skills, and abilities you would bring to the position. Let's say that a government hiring manager—Colonel Mustard—is looking to hire a federal investigator to join his top-notch team of patriotic detectives. The colonel has a very long list of KSAs and career experiences that will be needed by his new private eye. The colonel jots down his job description with quill and pen and submits it to the HR team to place into a job vacancy announcement on the USAJOBS website. Lo and behold, Colonel Mustard has hundreds of applicants vying to be the next federal investigator. Colonel Mustard would love to hire all of his top candidates, however he must adhere to his budget, and he only has funding to hire one superstar investigator. The colonel's HR staff is now faced with the daunting task of narrowing down the hundreds of candidates to a cadre of highly qualified candidates. The HR staff rates and ranks each candidate's résumé to identify which future crime fighter has the qualifications and KSAs to get the job done.

CIVIL SERVANTS: COMPETITIVE VERSUS EXCEPTED SERVICE

Civil Servant
The term *civil servant* refers to any member of the federal workforce. This includes all persons managed (and paid by) the US government, with the exception of active-duty, reserve, and National Guard members of the US Army, Navy, Air Force, Coast Guard, and Marine Corps.

Competitive Service
Job postings in the competitive service are filled through competition among applicants. HR staff will rate and rank applicants based on OPM regulatory requirements, and those applicants with the highest scores will move forward to the next step in the application process.

Excepted Service
Excepted service refers to civil service positions and agencies that do not fall under the requirements of OPM. Excepted service agencies determine their own qualifications

and job requirements and are not subject to the same classification, appointment, selection, or pay rules of the competitive service.

If you enter into civil service as an excepted service employee, you cannot use your excepted service position to give you leverage into the competitive service. For example, let's say you applied for and were offered an excepted service position at the GS-11 level. After one year, you want to apply for a promotion to the GS-12 level in the competitive service. The competitive service will not recognize your work history at the excepted service GS-11 level because you didn't go through their competitive process. You will have to compete for the competitive service GS-12 position.

If you competed for, were selected, and accepted a competitive service position at the GS-12 level, once you have passed the probationary period in that position (usually one year), you will be eligible for a GS-13 position in the competitive service. You do not have to go through the process to "compete" for a GS-12 again since you already competed once (and got the job!) and have successfully completed your probationary period. Sometimes because of the less stringent requirements, it can be easier to enter into federal employment through an excepted service agency or appointment. The challenge comes if you decide to move from excepted service to competitive service, although some agencies have reciprocal agreements to make the transition seamless for employees.

Reporting Your Findings

We must teach our children to resolve their
conflicts with words, not weapons.
—William J. Clinton

The hard-working folks at the US State Department pride themselves with protecting the lives and interests of US citizens abroad. There is much more to the State Department than meets the eye. These employees may best be known for their work in foreign embassies and their foreign-aid efforts, but there are many more positions helping run the show behind the scenes.

Just like the Olympic flame, many employees of the US State Department are well traveled. When it comes to a monumental international event like the Olympics, dozens of US diplomats and other officials are oiling the gears of this multicultural machine. Consular officers assist American athletes and their family members with travel and passport services. Security experts look after the safety needs of US athletes and tackle any sign of security threats. Public affairs officers and their staff engage in sports diplomacy and prepare members of the US delegation and Team USA for a whirlwind of media interviews.

US FUN FACT

The Winter Olympic Games would not be possible if it were not for historic patents created by American inventors such as the hockey stick and the snowboard. If you have an invention of your own or want to work on cutting-edge products and technologies, check out careers with the United States Patent and Trademark Office (USPTO.gov).

Just like State Department employees and Olympic athletes, you have had a multitude of challenges, experiences, opportunities, and achievements in your career. Your current goal is to communicate these accomplishments on your federal résumé.

Brainstorm

Before building your résumé, it is wise to take the time to brainstorm about your best and brightest career moments. These moments emphasize accomplishments you have made, changes you have initiated, processes you have improved, revenue you have produced, teams you have led, training you have conducted, volunteer work you have managed (or engaged in), and awards you have earned.

CAREER CLUE

If you find it difficult to boast about your skills, meet a friend, family member, colleague, classmate, fellow soldier, or former supervisor for coffee to discuss what they think your best traits and talents are. You'll probably be pleasantly surprised!

Multitalented

When choosing from your assortment of abilities and array of achievements, it is best to provide a variety of valuable skill sets, showing you are a highly qualified candidate—and a well-rounded individual. By reviewing the KSAs (found under the "Qualifications and Evaluations" tab in the vacancy announcement), you will know what the hiring team is seeking. Weave these KSAs into your résumé to create a seamless document that gives the hiring team exactly what it requires.

Be Specific

By using specific dollar amounts, numerical values, statistics, timetables, and percentages, you are able to paint a tangible picture for the hiring team to assess and appreciate. You want to represent your skills in a way that portrays depth and breadth of experience at the highest level possible. Do not use examples that do not capture you in your most positive light—unless it is to prove your strengths in the face of adversity.

Create Your Own STAR Stories

Using the following formula, identify two to three project success stories for each position you've held in the past ten years.

★ Situation	What was the project/assignment and what was the backstory or backdrop?
★ Task	For which tasks were you personally responsible—and what was your role?
★ Action	What actions did you take to resolve the situation?
★ Result	What was the outcome as a result of your efforts in the project/assignment?

These short-story "STAR" accomplishments will be incorporated into your federal résumé to help prove your career competence. Documenting these successes will also help prepare you for the federal interview and any future writing assignments throughout your federal hiring process.

It is best to document all requested and required skills and abilities in order for your application to move forward in the hiring process.

SAMPLE STAR RESPONSE

Situation (S)

Advertising revenue was falling off for my college newspaper, *The Gov Review*, and large numbers of long-term advertisers were not renewing contracts.

Task (T)

My goal was to generate new ideas, materials, and incentives that would result in at least a 15 percent increase in advertisers from the previous year.

Action (A)

I designed a new promotional packet to go with the rate sheet and compared the benefits of *The Gov Review* circulation with other advertising media in the area. I also set up a special training session for the account executives with a School of Business Administration professor who discussed competitive selling strategies.

Result (R)

As a result of my efforts, *The Gov Review* signed contracts with fifteen former advertisers for daily ads and five for special supplements. We increased our new advertisers by 20 percent over the same period in the previous year.

TEN STAR EXAMPLES

Communications

As an undergraduate student at the ABC State University from September 2008 to the present, I produced a minimum of five research papers each semester. These were technical papers that present and support a thesis statement, providing detailed documentation to justify my position. In my senior year, I produced a twenty-five-page paper that explored the issue of public health systems in Europe and their possible application in this country. My paper received a grade of 98 percent and was published in the School of Public Administration's newsletter.

Development

In my position as director of development for ABC Company from May 2008 to June 2012, I directed the creation of all marketing materials for federal defense industry marketing. I created complex technical proposals, often comprising many volumes and thousands of pages of highly technical data. I prepared the introduction and abstract portions of these proposals, synthesizing the information to create an informative overview of the contents in order to convey the information to nontechnical management officials. These proposals were instrumental in securing new corporate business totaling $1.5 million, and I consistently received bonuses of up to $20,000 based upon my performance.

Financial Management

In my role as financial management specialist for XYZ Company from June 2010 to January 2014, I was selected to assist in transferring 1,800 employees from location

A to location B, ensuring that all their administrative needs would be handled. I was tasked with overseeing the final leg of the time line and working with my colleagues to calculate and coordinate the additional services required by the massive influx of employees. These included services in the areas of IT, contracting, facilities, human resources, security, and equal-employment opportunity. I developed budget models to present to senior-level management that showed the burden shift and the available options for meeting their administrative needs. As a result of my effort and budget projections, the final leg of the transfer went smoothly, and XYZ Company was successful in attaining the additional resources and employees required to effectively service the new employees.

Administrative Specialist

In my role as administrative specialist with ABC Realty, I designed and developed an electronic tracking system. The database I designed allowed me to track all transactions in process. In a real estate environment, each activity must be completed in order and by the dates outlined in the contract or clients could be found negligent and in breach of their contract. I planned the changeover, created a system that would work for all parties, input all data in the new system, and trained the remaining realtors in the office. As a result of my efforts, office staff was better able to manage competing demands and efficiency increased. Additionally, the chances of contract breaches decreased significantly, and my supervisor rewarded me for taking the initiative to develop the system with a $2,000 bonus.

Principal Broker/Manager

In my role at XYZ Realty as the principal broker/manager, I was responsible for planning and developing a start-up division that focused on commercial sales and leasing. Part of the analysis involved conducting several studies to determine the best target markets and the approaches that should be undertaken by XYZ Realty. I generated a cost-benefit analysis for the effectiveness of the company outreach activities in its other components. Using this analysis, I made company marketing decisions that involved the creation of a new, innovative system for reaching out to the community in an organized fashion on a weekly basis. Using several electronic mechanisms, such as Co-Star, Loop Net, Globe Street, and others, I developed a successful strategy for reaching out to the brokerage community for purchasing, selling, leasing, and trading the company holdings. Under my leadership, the realty division has been extremely successful in executing work priorities since its inception, which now boasts transactions valued in excess of $30 million.

Manager

In my role as ABC branch manager from April 2009 to present, I found that there were no systems in place for managers at various levels of the organization to communicate on a routine basis and in an organized manner. I presented to my senior management team the concept of a forum through which various levels of management would meet. I worked with my supervisor and his colleagues to develop this forum for managers to meet face-to-face, conduct high-level discussions of pressing issues, and share challenges that needed to be addressed. This forum was named the ABC Liaison Council, and it currently has more than ten members attending. As a result of my leadership in establishing this forum, quarterly meetings have been held over the past eighteen months. Managers now feel more supported and are welcoming and receiving more visits from corporate senior-level managers. All managers now have improved understanding of other management perspectives and have significantly improved communication. This forum has dramatically increased the quality of the relationship between managers and senior-level management.

Research Management Consultant

I solved a large and complex problem while serving as a research management consultant (June 2008 to May 2010) for a major industry-research program. Specifically, the association's research program was implemented by ten work groups composed of scientific experts and managed by contract staff. Our client needed to ensure that all these work groups were following the appropriate processes, documenting their decisions, securing the necessary approvals, and following up appropriately with applicants and peer reviewers. I needed to figure out how they could do that. First, I designed and produced a series of brief question-and-answer format guidance documents ("cheat sheets") for the scientific work groups that explained the key research management processes (such as requests for proposals [RFP], conducting peer review, and developing research agreements). Next, I designed an award package summary sheet to be utilized by the scientific work groups. This tool documented all necessary processes in a single document, providing one place for the work group to summarize any unusual circumstances that arose with a particular RFP. Finally, I designed a series of logs that allowed the association to track various paperwork-heavy processes (such as external peer review). These logs enabled both the association and contract staffs to ensure that peer reviewers completed the necessary paperwork (such as confidentiality agreements) prior to receiving research proposals for review. The logs also ensured that peer reviewers were paid promptly for their services. The result of my efforts was that the scientific work groups and contract staff used the "cheat sheets" enthusiastically. They found them much easier to understand than the lengthy research-management manual that had been issued previously. Consequently, work groups began using more uniform processes.

Computer Specialist

In my role as a computer specialist at USDA from September 2005 to July 2010, USDA partnered with XYZ University to develop mapping software (Geographical Information System). I was tasked with gathering and analyzing information to present to management to allow them to make an informed decision regarding the project's implementation. I gathered pertinent information through a thorough literature review, face-to-face interviews, trend and best-practices research, and conducting a survey. My information analysis allowed me to develop options with recommendations for management to consider. I created a flowchart and decision matrix of the status quo and designed several option charts showing my proposed recommendations. As a result of my ability to gather thorough information with which USDA senior-level managers could make decisions, they decided to move forward with the project, purchasing a commercial off-the-shelf product and customizing it to meet USDA business objectives.

Management Analyst

In my role as management analyst from May 2010 to June 2014, I was responsible for preparing 217 separate reports for the department's program offices in support of the Federal Human Capital Survey. The challenging aspect of this assignment was the time line and the detail required for completing the reports. The program offices were eager to get their results because they were developing strategic initiatives that would cascade from the data I was providing to them. I was able to deliver accurate data to the program offices, and I was successful in meeting my assigned deadline.

Training Specialist

In my role as training specialist from August 2010 to present, I was tasked with analyzing the problems associated with training regional office employees in mandatory subject matter, as determined by headquarters. This was challenging because of the training implementation time line and associated budget constraints. I gathered data relative to headquarters' goals and objectives, such as budget projections, travel expenses, training delivery evaluations, and other types of data. I analyzed the data and developed viable options for senior-level management. I created recommendations for senior-level management in the form of a report and flowchart that mapped out the various options. Although the time line was tight, the training was successfully released to three hundred employees in thirteen regions using my recommended method with strong positive results.

CHAPTER 6

Putting the Pieces Together: Your Federal Résumé

Believe you can and you're halfway there.
—President Theodore Roosevelt

Each and every day, we are surrounded by waves of energy known as the *electromagnetic spectrum*. The frequency and wavelength of these waves make up every sound we hear and sight we see—and there are far more wavelengths present that our limited human senses simply cannot process or comprehend. The wavelengths that we can see generate visible light and color in our world. However, the waves that remain unseen still hold purpose.

You are the proud proprietor of a sensational spectrum of professional experiences. Some are stronger than others, some are more noteworthy than others, some are easily seen, and others remain hidden from the world. Your goal when creating a vivid and vibrant federal résumé is to make certain that all of your knowledge, skills, and abilities are visible in your federal application materials. This means that the position requirements as they relate to you and your work experience must be documented on your federal résumé. This will ensure that you and the federal HR hiring team are on the same wavelength. In other words, if it is not documented on your résumé, you don't get credit in the HR rating and ranking process.

Electromagnetic Spectrum
Source: NASA

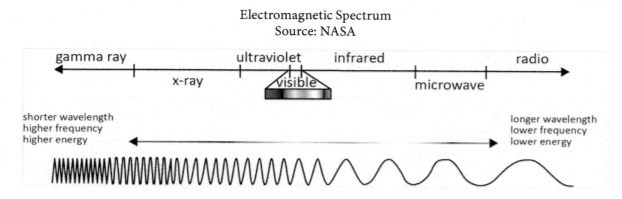

Low Frequency

Let's take a quick look at your core competencies and basic skill sets. Traditionally, simple proficiencies such as typing, answering phones, using a shovel, drafting e-mails, or lifting heavy objects are left out of a résumé. We would agree that these conventional tasks should remain assumed or unstated in a corporate setting. However, if the federal job qualifications section requires you to type thirty-five words per minute (WPM) or be able to lift fifty-plus pounds on a daily basis, make certain to dedicate space in your résumé to state these skills. This concept also applies to basic computer skills, programs, and software; do not assume that the hiring team already knows your basic talent aptitudes.

High Frequency

Your résumé may be satiated with prominent professional titles—manager, chief operating officer, principal, major general, or colonel. You may have received an advanced degree from Harvard or Yale, and your last name may be followed by MBA or PMP—or preceded by Dr. or Reverend. Please note that no matter how impressive your profession may be, the federal government will not hire you on title alone. You will need to provide significant—visible—evidence within your résumé that you have performed the duties in the job announcement (at about 80 percent), not just that you think you can do the work (even if you are sure you can). If the announcement requires ten years of experience in managing teams, the capability to manage multimillion-dollar budgets, and familiarity with Six Sigma training and practices, then be certain to highlight your experience in these precise areas on your federal résumé.

Let's put this information together into the building blocks that will form your federal résumé. Below is some information that should get you started on the right track as you start to draft your federal résumé.

The Differences

The federal résumé is completely different from the private/corporate sector résumé in a number of ways. Here is a list of the most common differences:

PRIVATE-SECTOR RÉSUMÉ	FEDERAL RÉSUMÉ
1–2 Pages	An average of 5 pages long
Functional, creative, or graphic allowed	Traditional reverse-chronological order
Bullet points	Description of details in full phrases or sentences
Succinct career highlights	Informative descriptions
Few details	Extensive details with keywords that explain your job qualifications
Business-focused	Agency-, program-, and services-focused
Profit-driven	Budget-driven, results-driven
Customer and client consumers	General public or segment of public
Product or service	Program or service
Support for customers and clients	Comply with regulations
Service to customers and clients	Service and information to the US population

THE MUST-HAVES

Five-Page Résumé

One of the most astounding differences between corporate and federal résumés is length. The average federal résumé is five pages long. This is because of the level of detail required by the federal HR team. They are giving you a rating based on a set of criteria for the job you are targeting. They compare those criteria with your résumé. The more information they identify on your résumé, the more credit you get in this process—and the higher the level of job you will qualify for. Details such as how you accomplished the work, what skills you used, and the process you engaged in are extremely important for your rating.

Reverse Chronological (Chronological)

Federal résumés are written in reverse chronological order; your most recent job will appear at the top of your résumé, and you will work backward from there. This is the easiest way for the HR team to see that you meet the minimum qualification standards (the twelve-month requirement). If you provide them with any other format (such as functional), it is extremely difficult for them to give you credit for the twelve-month-minimum-experience requirement.

One Decade

The government is looking for you to convey the last ten years of experience in your résumé. If you don't yet have ten years of experience, then go back as far as you can. If you have more than ten years of experience and within the last ten years you can convey at least twelve months of experience for the job you are targeting, you only need to go back ten years. If you have more than ten years of work experience, but the experience you want to show on your résumé is beyond the ten-year mark, go back ten years chronologically. Anything beyond the ten-year mark should be placed in a separate section after the last chronological job you held ("Additional Information"). In this new section, list your experience that relates to your target job and the number of total years of experience you gained in that work experience. It is not necessary to list the chronological dates. (Please note that there are a handful of agencies that will ask for the applicant to list all relevant work experience and this may require going back further than 10 years; check the announcement for details).

Repetition

Because of the crediting-plan process, repetition is encouraged. If you did the work and have the skills, they should be listed in each job on your résumé. In this manner, you are sure to receive the credit you deserve for your experience.

Achievements and Accomplishments

Let's take a quick joyride down memory lane to assess your personal career highlights and achievements. If you suffer from a severe case of modesty, you may want to bring a friend or colleague along for this ride. A second driver may help you see some things you may not have seen—and help you eliminate some personal blind spots. The STAR format (see chapter 5) is a great format for documenting your accomplishments. Here are a few questions to get you started on the right path:

- What skills do/did you use in your job?
- What roles do/did you play?
- What tasks have you mastered?
- What value did you add to your organization?
- What projects have you led or participated in?
- What was the last award for which you were nominated?

Below is a checklist of information that you should compile to get you started on writing your federal résumé.

Employment/Work/Service History

Document your professional experience for the last ten years, listing each of your jobs with month and day started and month and day finished. Include your job title, company/organization name, salary, and supervisor name and contact information. Although salary and supervisor information are optional unless stated as mandatory in the job announcement, it is best to compile this information during your initial gathering session. In as much detail as possible, document what you did at each position. Make sure this information is comprehensive and detailed in terms of the skills you gained/used and the responsibility you held. The major focus will be on the last two to four jobs, depending on how relevant they each are. Keep these questions in mind throughout the documentation process:

- What skills did I use?
- How did I do the work?
- What challenges did I overcome? How did I overcome them?
- How did I communicate with others?
- For what was I responsible?

Education, Certifications, and Licensures

Gather information about your university or college education, along with your major(s) and minor(s). If you have not graduated, gather information on the number of semester hours toward completion of your degree. You can include your GPA if you desire. If you are using education to qualify you for the job, an unofficial transcript will be required. Later in the hiring process, you may be asked to furnish an official copy. If you have a certification or licensure, you will need to document the organization from which you received it and any other pertinent information.

Accomplishments

For each job you held, you will want to identify two to three major accomplishments you were responsible for creating. Writing these accomplishments using the STAR formula (see chapter 5) can be beneficial for use in your résumé and for preparing for your federal interview. These should document things you have done, accomplishments you have achieved, changes you have implemented, or processes you have improved. They bring validity to your set of skills.

One of the best ways to think about which accomplishments to document is to review several target vacancy announcements and identify the skills for which they are looking. These can serve as a guide to determine which topics you may want to cover in your accomplishments. Use specific time, dollar, or numerical values whenever possible to show the depth and breadth of your experience at the highest possible level.

Endorsements

If you have any recommendations or endorsements from colleagues, clients, or supervisors, you can include a few sentences in your résumé. This can be accomplished by using a letter of recommendation, performance reviews, or LinkedIn. Once you have created a LinkedIn profile, you can ask others to provide you with endorsements electronically. Then copy and paste them into your federal résumé once it is complete.

Other Information

You will need to identify and document your technical skills, computer skills, language skills, publications, presentations, and awards and honors. If you would like to include information on relevant volunteer work, community service, special activities, or memberships, gather information on these activities. Depending on your role in these organizations, you may wish to give a brief description of your activities. If you were or are in the military, you will want to gather your performance reviews (OERs or fitness reports), Defense Department Form 214 (DD-214) if you have already separated, or if you are still on active duty, a working copy of your DD-214 or a statement of service from personnel. If you have a service-connected disability of 30 percent or more, documentation will be required, generally received from the US Department of Veterans Affairs.

GETTING STARTED

Job Descriptions

For each job you have held over the past ten years, you will want to document in detail the work you performed along with the depth and breadth of your experience. Use your current private-sector résumé, organizing it chronologically (with your most recent job listed first). Your goal is to document as much information as you can about your skills, competencies, duties, and relevant job information.

Use the USAJOBS website to locate several vacancy announcements in your target job series. From these vacancy announcements, copy the text that applies to you from the "Duties" and "Qualifications and Evaluations" tabs into a separate document. Incorporate as much of this text as you can into your federal résumé. Do not copy and paste the text exactly from the vacancy announcement. Your résumé needs to be true based on your background, and the federal HR team will know if you have copied text from the vacancy announcement and pasted it into your résumé.

To quickly identify key words from the vacancy announcement, copy and paste text from the "Duties" and "Qualifications and Evaluations" sections of the vacancy announcement and paste them into the Tagcrowd website (Tagcrowd.com). Those words that appear in large and bold font are key words you will want to incorporate into your résumé. Below is an example:

The structure of the job description should capture the federal HR team's attention. To do this, we recommend breaking down the job description section into about six to eight paragraphs or "sound bites" of no more than about eight to ten lines each. The first paragraph in the section should be a summary overview of the job duties and responsibilities for that particular job. For example:

> Program Manager: Effectively managed and maintained all logistical aspects for airline operation, including customer service, operational safety, security, performance, airport community relations, and human capital development. Provided direct oversight in a matrixed environment for comprehensive program responsibilities, implementing effective program and project management techniques and logistics analysis. Oversaw the project plans, implementation, success, and compliance for quality customer service, operational performance, human capital, financial affairs, and safety and security.

The subsequent paragraphs should be a breakdown of the summary paragraph, broken down into key roles you played in each job (often called *core skills*). If you think about the roles that you played in each job (or the many "hats" that you wore in terms of responsibilities), these roles should be documented in the paragraphs after the summary paragraph. It is strongly recommended that each of these paragraphs be labeled in a manner that will allow the federal HR team to quickly identify the core skills you performed. The labels you select should align with the key words and action verbs found in the target vacancy announcements. For example:

> HUMAN RESOURCES OVERSIGHT: Managed and coordinated personnel activities to meet organizational business needs. Used expert knowledge of HR law and policies to support full life cycle approach to staffing, job analysis, recruitment, compensation, classification, employee relations, workforce planning, and training activities for fifty management and nonmanagement positions. Directed and coordinated all aspects of airport operation to meet and exceed corporate goals, while fostering high-quality external and internal customer service teams. Served as a strategic business partner, fulfilling personnel requirements at every level.

> FINANCIAL MANAGEMENT / BUDGETING: Developed and administered an annual budget of $58 million. Supervised business unit finances. Planned, coordinated, and developed cost estimates and engaged in strategic analysis to support short- and

long-term funding strategies. Developed and implemented long-term objectives, priorities, and other resource requirements for airline operations, human capital management, safety and security, and customer service planning and execution.

CONDUCTED AUDITS AND ENSURED COMPLIANCE WITH REGULATIONS: Performed station monthly, quarterly, and annual audits related to financial transactions, safety, and security compliance. Ensured compliance with regulations with the Environmental Protection Agency, Occupational Safety and Health Administration, Federal Aviation Administration, Transportation Security Agency, and Food and Drug Administration.

INTERPRETED REGULATIONS AND POLICIES OF A HIGHLY TECHNICAL NATURE and recommended solutions to unique challenges. Translated complex regulatory information into guidance for employees. Maintained up-to-date knowledge of policies and regulations affecting program operations. Ensured that information systems complied with legislative and regulatory requirements for the design, development, security, and maintenance of the sensitive and timely data that formed the basis for the airline operations center, customer service, employee relations, and financial-management systems.

SENSITIVE DATA COORDINATOR: Appointed airline representative for sensitive security data sharing with federal agencies and intelligence communities to mitigate security threats. Served as the principal ground security coordinator, responsible for disseminating information to direct reports on sensitive security information, security directives, and bulletins. Oversaw the control of secure identification display area and compliance of the Aircraft Operator Standard Security Program.

Accomplishments

Accomplishments give the federal HR team a solid example of how you were able to use your skills to create results in your work environments. Using the STAR formula (see chapter 5) document at least two accomplishments for each job you've held. Your accomplishments should support the information you are providing (skills, duties, and responsibilities). For example:

Created an employee tracking system tool that provided supervisors with a method to effectively monitor and follow up on attendance issues. Resulted in a sudden and significant improvement and effectively established accountability. Reduced biweekly payroll processing time by 70 percent and payroll clerk's productivity increased. As a result of improved payroll reporting, the corporation averaged $3,000 in monthly cost savings.

KSA Statements

From the "Qualifications and Evaluations" section of your target vacancy announcement, you will need to identify the knowledge, skill, and ability (KSA) statements. It is your responsibility to ensure you are incorporating the KSAs into your résumé as statements or examples. Otherwise, you will not be deemed qualified—not because you don't have the KSAs but because you didn't describe them in your résumé. Below is a sample list of KSAs from a vacancy announcement. As an applicant, you are expected to address each of these statements in your résumé. For example:

- Experience developing and preparing reports
  Possible response: Synthesized data into succinct reports for supervisor. Trained and supervised junior staff to analyze data and develop reports.

- Experience evaluating programs and policies
  Possible response: Maintained up-to-date knowledge of policies and regulations affecting program operations. Conducted monthly program evaluations to ensure adherence to policy guidelines.

- Experience researching and analyzing data in order to develop processes and procedures.
  Possible response: Used analytical findings and technical expertise to develop and implement policies and procedures for operations.

Career Summary

This section represents an overview of who you are, the experience you bring, and your areas of expertise. It documents your career highlights. The job titles you are applying for should be prevalent in your professional profile along with key words from the vacancy announcement you are targeting. For example:

PROGRAM ANALYST / OPERATIONS MANAGER with more than 13 years of progressive experience providing analysis, strategic planning, program, and project management to government and public-sector organizations. Expertise in strategic and tactical planning, program, and management analysis and resource analysis/ optimization. Solid record of performance managing analytical studies, key initiatives, and high-profile performance improvement projects. Technical expert and analyst on complex program issues. Very strong critical-thinking, problem-solving, research, and liaison skills.

CLEARANCE: Understand the security clearance process and willing to complete.

AREAS OF EXPERTISE: Program evaluation and management; project lifecycle management; strategic and operations planning; human resources management; workforce analysis and planning; operational, financial, and compliance auditing; internal control reviews; process improvement and simplification; security and safety; emergency preparedness; team and project leadership; quantitative/ qualitative analysis; risk and feasibility assessment; technical, regulatory, and best-practices research; policy analysis; preparing press releases; and excellent oral and written communication skills.

TECHNICAL SKILLS: Microsoft Word, Excel, Access, PowerPoint; Oracle and Enterprise Revenue Planning financial systems. Corporate specific safety, asset inventory, and aircraft tracking and routing databases. Able to conduct credible research using the Internet.

ENDORSEMENTS: "Joe is a talented leader with a strong background. During his time on my team, Joe took on projects and completed them with little direction. He was given a task and completed it on time or early and in most cases exceeded expectations. Joe's work ethic is second to none. He sees a project through and owns the issue until resolved. Joe pays close attention to detail and ensures a thorough and realistic solution. Joe is an effective leader with the ability to pull together a strong team."

—Jeff Holmes, regional director, ABC Company, managed Joe at ABC Company

"Integrity, trust, dedication, honesty, perseverance, and adaptability. These are just a few of the many words that describe Joe's character and personality. I had the pleasure and honor of working with Joe who was consistently able to demonstrate that he can inspire and motivate any group of ordinary people to do extraordinary things."

Ben Brandt, general manager, XYZ Company

Additional Information

The additional information section of your federal résumé is where you can document experience that is more than ten years old, honors or awards you have received, community service or volunteer work you have performed, or any other relevant information you want to share on your résumé. For example:

ADDITIONAL WORK EXPERIENCE: More than five years of experience as a program coordinator for ABC Company.

HONORS AND AWARDS: Recipient of "employee of the month" for four out of twelve months in one year

Below is a sample federal résumé.

Alena Jackson

703-555-1212

mjackson@gmail.com

Work Experience

09/2005–Present, PROFESSIONAL PROFILE, Career Summary, 123 Home Street Avenue Street, Baltimore, MD 12345, Hours/week: 40

PROJECT AND PROGRAM MANAGER / ANALYST with more than 15 years of progressive experience providing analysis, strategic planning, program and project management. Expertise in strategic and tactical planning, program and management analysis, and resource analysis and optimization. Solid record of performance managing analytical studies, key initiatives, and high-profile performance improvement projects. Technical expert and analyst on complex program issues. Very strong critical-thinking, problem-solving, research, and liaison skills. Recognized for outstanding communication skills, flexibility, keen political savvy, sense of humor, and leadership abilities.

CLEARANCE: Understand the SF-86 and security clearance process; prepared to complete.

AREAS OF EXPERTISE: Program evaluation and management; project lifecycle management; educational leadership and training; strategic and operations planning; human resources management; workforce analysis and planning; operational, compliance auditing; internal control reviews; process improvement and simplification; financial oversight; budget forecasting, development, and planning; team and project leadership; quantitative/qualitative analysis; risk and feasibility assessment; technical, regulatory, and best-practices research; policy analysis; negotiating; marketing; and excellent oral and written communication skills.

TECHNICAL SKILLS: Microsoft Project; ActiveCollab; BaseCamp; Internet Marketing Tools and Processes; Google Analytics (Digital Analytics Fundamentals, Ecommerce Analytics Certified); Adobe (Creative Suite, Acrobat, Digital Editions); QuickBooks; Quicken; Microsoft (Word, Excel, PowerPoint, Publisher, Outlook); WordPress and Drupal Content Management; Basic HTML; MAC OS; Windows OS

ENDORSEMENTS:

"During her project manager role, Alena always executed at a high standard with enthusiasm and commitment. As a consulting associate, Alena was a true pillar during the financial-management process. Her ability to gather information and make strong business decisions was greatly appreciated. You could always count on her judgment during the crucial times. While working with Fiona in the project management capacity, I was always in awe regarding the creativity and innovation she brought—she has a knack for thinking outside the box and turning vision from paper to reality."

Norma Radar, chief executive assistant (customer of Alena)

"I highly recommend Alena Jackson. If your organization is looking to add quality resources, Alena brings tremendous energy, deep knowledge, and a fresh approach to the execution of tasks she is assigned. Commitment, integrity, passion, quality, and great service all define Alena. She possesses a strong work ethic and an overall serious countenance. She works well with other people and also individually. Yet, she is really more of a leader than a follower. She can manage and supervise other employees well, with little or no supervision."

Georgia Clifford, manager

01/2009—Present, CHIEF OPERATING OFFICER AND PROJECT MANAGEMENT CONSULTANT, Baltimore, MD, 123 Covington Street, Silver Spring, MD, Hours/week: 40, Salary: $75,000, Supervisor: Jane Doe, 410-456-8444

OPERATIONS AND PROJECT MANAGER: Oversee all ventures, tracking progress, issues, communication, escalations, and overall workflow to ensure timely delivery. Manage multiple projects, developing and maintaining project plans, while directing and motivating the work of others. Demonstrate expert knowledge of project management by applying various methods and techniques, to include: scope management; quality management; cost and schedule development and execution; work breakdown structure development; cost benefit analysis; feasibility studies; systems lifecycle management; human resources management; and integration management.

+++ Boosted productivity 50 percent after designing a system to support outsourcing overflow of web projects.

+++ Implemented improvement tools and processes that efficiently decrease time to completion.

+++ Wrote technical procedures and provided one-on-one training to not only the freelance contractors but also to clients on how to check status of their projects, through implemented platform and on internal process structure. This instilled a level of confidence that led to a $150,000 increase in the contract value.

ASSESS OPERATIONAL PRODUCTIVITY, EFFECTIVENESS, AND EFFICIENCY OF PROGRAM AND PROJECTS. Provide complex quantitative and qualitative analysis to measure project effectiveness and efficiency. Seek root causes of problems with organizational policies and processes and work to resolve them. Analyze data to determine compliance with established regulations and organizational policies, management principles, rules, and guidelines. Synthesize data into succinct reports to demonstrate needs to adjust policies and procedures. Provide risk analysis to determine potential courses of action.

PLAN AND IMPLEMENT ORGANIZATIONAL CHANGES within delegated authority to continually improve organizational outcomes and to increase effectiveness and efficiency of programs. Identify opportunities to combine innovation and technology to support business goals and objectives. Examine organizational goals and objectives to determine opportunities for developing policies, procedures, methods, and standards. Expert in exploiting the use of technology to improve operational effectiveness and efficiency.

+++ Successfully conceived, helped design and implemented platform through which external contractors could work on and report progress on projects they were assigned to do. This resulted in a 60 percent increase in production, 40 percent reduction in time lost due to multiple projects having to wait for work to begin, and improved responsiveness to customers on acquired projects.

FINANCE/BUDGET: Analyze need for human resource capital and various operations related to contract fulfillment and make recommendations to senior management on resource allocation. Provide revenue projections using computer applications and software. Adhere to budget guidelines for program expenses. Provide detailed monthly expense reports.

+++ Improved budget forecasting accuracy 60 percent by implementing financial systems and fine-tuning the data-input process

LEAD PEOPLE AND CROSS-FUNCTIONAL TEAMS: Provide leadership toward meeting vision, mission, and goals of an inclusive workplace that facilitates cooperation and teamwork, fosters the development of others, and supports constructive resolution of conflicts.

PROVIDE EXCELLENT CUSTOMER SERVICE through analysis of customer feedback and focus of attention on areas requiring improvement. Evaluate client needs and develop, plan, execute, and manage communication strategies. Develop and maintain positive relationships with clients, employees, contractors, and vendors.

+++ Improved customer service satisfaction by 3 percent annually and expanded client base 35 percent

ARTICULATE COMMUNICATOR: Summarize and communicate highly technical and complex information into clear, concise briefings and reports for senior-level management. Conduct meetings and provide presentations to groups and individual key stakeholders using appropriate software and superior communication skills. Write, edit, and present status reports, working papers, briefings, strategic plans, and proposals. Generate clear and succinct daily, weekly, monthly, and quarterly financial and forecasting reports.

BUILD AND MAINTAIN EFFECTIVE WORKING RELATIONSHIPS in a team environment. Collaborate with others to raise additional capital at appropriate valuations to enable the company to meet sales/growth objectives. Educate, advise, negotiate, collaborate, and build support for ideas and initiatives, tactfully and diplomatically addressing issues that are in contention or sensitive. Serve as expert liaison and establish high level of trust with and between corporate staff and clients.

03/2011—03/2013, PROJECT MANAGER, ABC Company, 123 Stevens Street, Glen Burnie, MD, Hours/week: 40, Salary: $65,000, Supervisor: John Doe, 410-844-4444

BUSINESS DEVELOPMENT: Established and managed successful bakery. Evaluated client needs and developed, planned, executed, and managed communication strategies. Analyzed, researched, and implemented processes and systems including legal requirements, order management, accounting, and inventory-management systems. Designed and established enhanced packaging methods to preserve product quality and ensure flawless delivery. Consistently exceeded performance goals through development of innovative action plans, project management, and stakeholder outreach.

MARKETING AND ANALYSIS: Defined market message, strategized about online marketing and advertising, and developed and executed the marketing plan. Conducted competitive analysis and adapted strategies and tactics in the marketplace for company growth. Conducted market analysis to capitalize on market trends. Conducted trend analyses and identified best practices in the field. Used knowledge gained to train employees and to increase organizational results. Developed reports using information compiled. Distinguished products in a market saturated with baked goods in order to promote exotic pastry line.

CUSTOMER SERVICE AND PROBLEM RESOLUTION: Formulated and executed ideas that resolved problems, improved business processes, and altered and expanded upon current products and services that produced measurable benefit to the organization and customer. Recognized by clients for exceptional customer service practices.

+++ Successfully demonstrated the ability to develop innovative customer service initiatives focusing on improving quality, anticipating risks and benefits while also balancing the interests of the customer in a multifaceted organization.

FINANCIAL MANAGEMENT: Researched and established competitive pricing for products and services. Formulated and tracked vending sales trends, gross and net profit margin, and return on investment. Budgeted for all expenditures including equipment, supplies, materials, maintenance, and related expenditures. Developed monthly reports to identify variances and unfunded needs.

RESULTS DRIVEN: APPLYING ACCOUNTABILITY, ENTREPRENEURSHIP, AND PROBLEM-SOLVING SKILLS, effectively met organizational goals and customer expectations. Made decisions that produced high-quality results by applying technical knowledge, analyzing problems, and calculating risks. Took into account a variety of complex factors and stayed alert to changing customer needs and challenges. Evaluated business successes and failures and applied lessons learned.

USED INTERPERSONAL SKILLS to establish and maintain professional working relationships. Utilized effective collaboration and coordination competencies to build trust and confidence in the company.

03/2010—01/2011, CONSULTING ASSOCIATE, XYZ Company, 1900 L St NW, Washington, DC 20036, Hours/week: 40, Salary: $55,000, Supervisor: Lacy Susan, 202-555-1234

PROJECT MANAGER: Collaborated with key federal and local agencies to define project scope, detail procedural plans, and implement operations within ten days of application submission. Collaborated with the Office of Economic Opportunity (OEO) to ensure effective project management procedures and delivered key financial management reporting. Designed project-specific corrective action plans, to enable "at-risk" projects to get back on track after a quarterly assessment of accounts and financial data for each project.

FINANCIAL REVIEW AND ANALYSIS: Monitored the allocation of $125 million in American Recovery and Reinvestment Act (ARRA) funds awarded to grant recipients in the Virgin Islands divided into 150 projects under various government agencies. Managed and led programs ensuring fiscal integrity and accountability and required information gathering. Interpreted and applied laws, regulations, policies, guidelines, and standard operating procedures in the implementation of budget and finance programs and activities. Compiled, analyzed, and synthesized financial data to identify trends and patterns in order to accurately forecast future funding availability as well as demonstrate past spending patterns. Applied fact-finding, analytical, and problem-solving methods and techniques to analyze applications, documentations, and reports.

+++ Created a very detailed and clear instructional manual on how to navigate complex financial management system used to track expenditure of funds that governed various and numerous steps needed to be taken to ensure figures were recorded correctly each month. As a result of my efforts, the manual is still being used as guidance to teach others how to navigate through management of their other projects.

+++ As part of preparation for audit, collected all facts, figures, and reports from various offices pertaining to the expenditure of funds. Printed off of the financial management system each monthly report and combined them in their proper order, and current labeling with tables of contents and indexes by government agencies into huge folders for presentation, a task which kept the small office of four working all through the night. As a result, the government of the United States Virgin Islands successfully passed the audit, 05/2010.

RISK MANAGEMENT: Supported the creation of a risk-management plan for the OEO. Generated and maintained risk-management process for opportunities and threats. Developed weekly issue and risk logs to monitor and track risk and action items and recommend contingencies to mitigate risks and issues. Performed ongoing review of program statuses during the transition period and identified risks. Documented the program progress including implementation, time lines, issues, risks, and successes. Assessed results and determined and implemented risk-mitigation solutions as appropriate.

USED COMPUTER APPLICATIONS, such as database management, word processing, and presentation software to produce a wide variety of materials and documents to include, but not limited to, briefings, spreadsheets, strategic plans, procedures, memoranda, correspondence, and presentations. Created document to track grant expiry, with an online visual time line tracker and created a scorecard review guidance document. Created flowcharts and graphics to convey complex information in easily understood format to audiences with varying levels of understanding of the topic. Updated the news and jobs sections of the OEO website, with the latest local ARRA-related news.

+++ Created an elaborate proposal document with an accompanying PowerPoint presentation proposal for client to present to her potential investors. After a review from the principal, the documents were passed on to the client who was very excited and happy. She presented them to her investors, in presentation folders I designed.

PERFORMED QUANTITATIVE AND STATISTICAL ANALYSIS as part of performance assessment to identify trends that led to programmatic improvements. Developed qualitative and quantitative methods to assess and evaluate assigned grant programs. Analyzed data to evaluate techniques, approaches, trends, and future requirements. Analyzed functions and workloads to determine staffing requirements. Developed new plans, schedules, and methods to accommodate changing requirements.

EXPERT PROBLEM-RESOLUTION SKILLS: Identified issues and developed new approaches to problems arising out of complex management areas. Proven expertise applying innovative thinking in conjunction with a technical understanding of emerging technologies to address needs and problems of providing services to a large organization. Reported, documented, and escalated performance issues and potential problems as soon as they occurred.

09/2005—05/2009, STUDENT AND TEAM LEADER / MEMBER, James Mason University, 111 Lindsey Court, Manassas, VA 20109, Hours/week: 40, Academic Advisor: Judy Fallsy

Received a master's degree in human resources management, 2009; a graduate certificate in e-commerce management, 2009; and a master's degree in project management, 2008.

PROJECT-COORDINATION SKILLS: Reviewed project requirements on business leadership and ethics to effectively delegate tasks and establish time lines. Demonstrated skill in defining project scopes and details. Created project plans by identifying tasks to be performed, necessary requirements, deliverables, and milestones. Recommended and devised individual scopes of work. Monitored results in alignment with project goals and objectives. Actively encouraged communication, coordination, innovation, and high-quality team products.

INDEPENDENTLY RESEARCHED AND ANALYZED highly complex policy, strategy, and conceptual issues involving current and past policies dealing with human resources and personnel management. Compiled and analyzed data to develop comprehensive research reports on finance and business practices. Summarized findings into concise briefings. Applied theory to business problems in dynamic global environments.

EDUCATION

Masters in human resources management, James Mason University

Bachelor of arts in history, University of Minnesota

JOB-RELATED TRAINING

Results-Based Management; Institutional Development and Capacity Building; Monitoring and Evaluating Projects; Logical Framework; Project Design; Environmental Impact Analysis

ADDITIONAL INFORMATION

ADDITIONAL RELEVANT WORK EXPERIENCE

+++ Department of Transportation (Financial Aviation Analysis), Washington, DC

INTERN: Monitored financial and economic conditions and status of various airlines. Created financial spreadsheets consisting of contrasts between competitive and financial issues of airlines (particularly those servicing Canada). Assisted in compiling and producing briefing papers for Secretary Peña of the Department of Transportation.

+++ Department of Treasury (Economic Policy), Washington, DC

PROJECT ASSISTANT: Assisted with tasks performed by twelve professional economists under director's supervision. Oversaw clerical and administrative duties concerning prospective interns and other job-opportunity applicants.

Follow the Clues

I walk slowly but I never walk backward.
—Abraham Lincoln

Federal agents have long used unconventional means to justify conventional ends. We all get a kick out of spy gadgets and their nifty tricks on the big screen, but have you ever taken a moment to ponder the role of peculiar inventions in our society? Tiny quirky gadgets like radio cufflink compasses, matchbox cameras, radio smoke pipes, coded makeup compacts, and silver dollar message holders have literally helped our country avoid international conflicts, win wars, and save lives. If your current federal job search is feeling more like a tedious lecture than an international spy flick, then maybe it is time to regroup, rethink, and repurpose your methods of career search. When you chow down at the salad bar, do you order a plain bowl of lettuce? When the flight attendant offers you a free seat upgrade to first class, do you stay in coach? You wouldn't limit your personal life, so why limit your career? Maybe you have been targeting a dream job at one of the major federal agencies such as the Department of State, Department of Energy, or Department of Defense, but you keep ending up empty-handed. These big pools attract big fish. Here are a few tips to help you swim upstream with just a few extra tweaks to your federal job search.

Think Outside the USA
Roughly 3.2 percent of the federal workforce performs its daily duties overseas. If you are at a stage in your life that allows you to travel abroad, you may want to consider a valuable employment experience overseas. The government provides state-of-the-art

language-immersion programs, and many foreign outposts even provide private schooling for the children of federal workers, military personnel, and diplomats. Civil servants working overseas may also receive additional or nontaxable pay, depending on their assigned location and job duties. Most agencies hold some presence overseas, however, specific agencies to target include the Department of Defense, Department of State, and US Agency for International Development (USAID).

Reverse Your Commute

For those persons living and working in metropolitan areas, a daily commute may steal hours of your life each day. While many persons apply for job opportunities directly in the city (Washington, DC, Atlanta, and Los Angeles), it may benefit you to search for gigs just outside the city limit (Arlington, Marietta, and Santa Monica). There may be less competition simply because other applicants may need to rely on public transportation, and you may also save time each day on your commute. Just remember to smile politely at those poor souls on the other side of the highway who are stopped in bumper-to-bumper traffic each morning—they haven't had their coffee yet.

Gulp—Contract Work

Government contracts may or may not hold the same weight and job security that they used to. With a questionable economy and a divided Congress, it is hard for many federal contractors to predict their future budgets, which, in due course, can hinder a company from executing its ideal hiring strategy. With that being said, performing contract work is one of the best ways to learn more about the federal arena. By working in a certain department or agency, you are able to build personal relationships and attain key skills needed in a government environment. When the time comes to "staff up" on the federal side, you may be in the running as a trusted colleague who can already perform the necessary functions of the job. Plus, your inside scoop will tune you into new directions and upcoming projects that may need federal staff in the future. Your contractor may be able to assist you in obtaining special training, certifications, computer skills, language lessons, or even a security clearance, any of which may be helpful in your quest for federal employment.

Temporary/Term Appointments

Even your know-it-all mother-in-law will tell you that you should test-drive the car or test out that mattress before making a final purchase. So why not test out a great career opportunity? A previous employee may have retired sooner than expected, resigned, or gone on extended personal or medical leave. If a special project is being adopted or a program is closing out, there may be a dire need for excellent teammates to ensure a successful transition. Whatever the reason, do not be intimidated by a temp or term position. Many temporary federal positions go for one-year increments—with the possibility of multiple annual extensions. A temp or term appointment is a great way to get your foot in the door (literally). But look carefully at the benefits since they may differ from those of permanent positions. You may search for these positions using the key word search feature in the USAJOBS website.

Direct Hire

These are jobs the government is desperate to fill, and the hiring process may be expedited and less stringent. Generally, they involve information technology, information security, and contract specialist positions, but there can be others. You may search for these positions using the key word search feature in the USAJOBS website.

Money Talks

The federal job landscape changes with the tides of budget and legislation. Our advice is to follow the money if you want to discover where the jobs are. If you can identify the entity receiving funding, then you will find an organization with money in its coffers—a budget that will allow them to hire new top talent—just like you.

CAREER CLUE

Following the federal money trail allows you to see which departments, initiatives, programs, and projects are receiving government funding. Stay on top of your current events in budget, programs, and legislation by visiting the White House, Senate, or Treasury websites (WhiteHouse.gov, Senate.gov, or Treasury.gov).

Follow The Legislation

Some legislation makes the front page of the newspapers (or blogs), while others simply pass without major public notice. Either way, each bill that passes both the House and Senate becomes a federal mandate for a new direction in federal time, effort, and funds. Authorized budget dollars will be allocated to distribute as needed to maintain compliance with ever-changing federal regulations. It is safe to say that the Farm Bill will form new jobs in agriculture, the Defense Authorization Act will establish new roles in the national security arena, and the Affordable Care Act will create careers in the health care field. You can stay informed about upcoming legislation buzz by visiting the Senate website.

Follow the Programs

When following the federal dollar, it is important to note which projects are up and coming and which are nearing the end of their life cycles. For example, if you have a science background, you may want to steer your career away from the NASA space shuttle program (now retired) and move toward asteroid detection, robotics, and human space exploration. You can even dig a bit deeper by following grant money— locating colleges, universities, or businesses that have been awarded government funds. By visiting your agency website of choice, you can learn about successful state-of-the-art programs, projects, and missions in your field of interest.

For example, the American Recovery and Reinvestment Act (ARRA), an $840 billion stimulus bill, injected funds into various areas, such as education, transportation, and health and human services. By keeping your ear to the pavement, you easily track any budget, reinvestment, aid, bailout, or stimulus. Based on information compiled by the US General Services Administration, below is a table of AARA funds awarded.

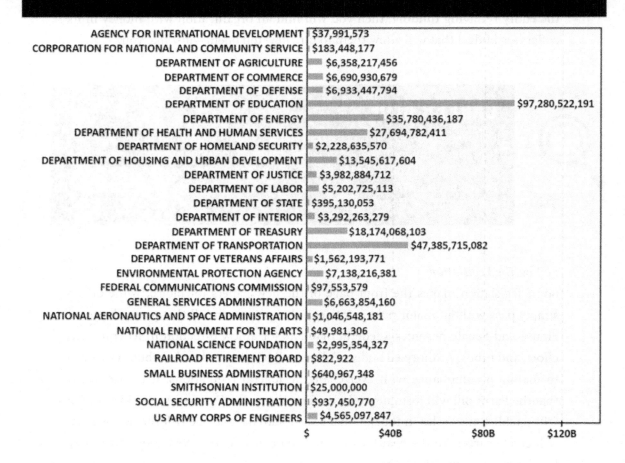

Starting Your Own Business

All US government agencies are required to give contractors a fair shake when it comes time to award new contract work. A certain percentage of contracts must be awarded to small businesses—particularly those owned and operated by veterans, women, and minorities. If you do not fall into one of these three categories, do not be discouraged; there are still many opportunities for all small-business owners. You may also want to consider partnering with a friend or colleague with military service or another specialty background. There is a plethora of information on business creation available at the Business USA website (Business.USA.gov), covering everything from business licensing to tax breaks. If you have a special talent or skill set to share, and would like to do so on your own terms, then bidding for a federal contract may be just the opportunity for which you've been looking.

US FUN FACT

There are five states with no sales tax: Alaska, Delaware, Montana, New Hampshire, and Oregon. Seven states have no income tax: Alaska, Florida, Nevada, South Dakota, Texas, Washington, and Wyoming.

Research and Development

Do not be afraid to revisit your findings, especially if you add a new skill or certification to your résumé. The research scientists at the US Department of Transportation consistently reassess their data, hoping to add improvements to their V2V technology, both in policy and technological advancements. Your initial job research is a foundation for building your future career.

The Cover Letter

*I am a great believer of luck, and I find the
harder I work, the more I have of it.*
—Thomas Jefferson

Cover letters are not required in the federal application process. In most cases, the HR staff cannot use cover letters for official documentation; they can only use your résumé. It is recommended you include them if they are mandatory (duh!), or if you are applying to an internship, or something similar. We like to include cover letters *if they are done correctly.*

If you choose to include a cover letter in your application package, make sure to put in the effort that will give you the greatest return on investment—and the most bang for your buck. This letter should be no longer than one page in length and should highlight three to five primary reasons why you are the very best candidate for the job. It should be individualized, personalized, and thoughtfully written. Generalized cover letters with canned language will not separate you from the competition. If you are applying to a position for which a cover letter is mandatory, or you've decided you'd like to include one, here are some tips for how to communicate to the hiring team that you are a serious candidate who is interested and qualified for the job.

The first building step is to lay out a firm foundation for your cover letter. Start with a personalized salutation and continue on to craft a unique introductory sentence that can grab attention, cultivate interest, and maybe even inspire *mystery*! Contrary to popular belief, your cover letter should never begin with "To Whom It May Concern" (bet you were bored just reading that). Most vacancy announcements on the USAJOBS website actually provide you with an HR point of contact (POC). Use it! When a name is not provided, go the extra mile and call the phone number provided to ask them to whom the cover letter should be addressed. The hiring team may be impressed by your immediate initiative, and they may even remember your name when the time comes to make big hiring decisions (long shot, but you never know).

COVER LETTER TIPS	
Be unique	Focus on the agency's needs
One page	Clean layout/design
Show motivation	Perfect grammar/spelling
Portray passion	Tout your talent
Explain your skills	State your next steps

SAMPLE COVER LETTER #1

Dear Ms. Defense:

Please accept my application for the administrative support assistant, serving the Department of Defense, Defense Health Agency, announcement #NCJT1442926012794764. Below are a few key reasons why I believe my skills and experience are an excellent fit for this role:

YOUR REQUIREMENTS	MY QUALIFICATIONS
Carry out the instructions of the director in an effective and timely fashion.	Experienced in working with executives, managing their schedules and department expense and/or department reports.
Ability to work tactfully with people; possess thorough knowledge of government operations.	Experienced deputy clerk with the Alexandria Circuit Court. Familiar with the judicial system and all Circuit Court government rules and regulations.
Knowledge of standard office practices and procedures, equipment, and clerical techniques.	More than five years of office experience; receptionist, office manager, and senior project manager. Performed full range of clerical duties and responsibilities for more than ten years.
Speak effectively to the public; investigate and recommend alternative funding sources such as grants and donations that would assist the department.	Trained in public speaking through Toastmasters International. Keynote speaker at a graduation ceremony. Performed research for funding and development for a major hospital improvements project.

Strong management skills and the ability to develop a purchasing team. Administrative and secretarial work.	Excellent leadership abilities and believe in employee participation and empowerment. Believe in independent work and collaborative teamwork to develop and produce effective ideas for department.
Must be customer-service and team oriented.	Passionate about providing the best possible customer service—five years of experience as a customer service manager. Managed more than twenty employees and raised over $2,500 in Children's Miracle Network funds, becoming number one in the company region.

I would appreciate the opportunity to meet with you in person to discuss your vision for this position. I will follow up with you next week to ensure receipt of my application materials.

Sincerely,
Susan B. Anthony

Sample Cover Letter #2

Dear Ms. Tubman:

With two years project analyst experience, two years classroom teaching experience (Biology, American History), and eight-plus years of project management, it is my hope that you will find me to be an excellent fit for the position of program analyst at the US Department of Education (#DOE123XYZ).

- Education Knowledge—Master's of education plus two years classroom teaching experience
- Microsoft Office Suite—Certified in MS Outlook, Word, Excel, PowerPoint, and MS Project
- Project Experience—Two years project analyst experience, eight years campaign management
- PMP Certification—Successfully completed NASA-PMP certification course
- Background Check—USIS Investigator (two years)—Top Secret Security Clearance

Project Coordination

As a project analyst for NASA, I had the thrill (and challenge) of coordinating project phases across time zones, cultures, and continents. After diving through a sea of acronyms, technical writing, budget snafus, and ever-changing policy and information technology (IT) systems, I was able to organize step-by-step solutions for NASA civil servants, contractors, and third-party vendors by troubleshooting, risk management, and promoting best practices across NASA's four mission directorates. *Ask me about a "day in the life" of a NASA project analyst!*

Hot off the Presses

With eight years of political campaign experience, I have had the joy of drafting, editing, and distributing newsworthy and time-sensitive press releases to thousands of media outlets across the globe. In addition to designing press packets, I enjoy creating e-mail marketing campaigns, web copy, blog posts, letter and postcard correspondence, newsletters, magazine articles, and social media copy (Facebook, Twitter, LinkedIn). *Ask me about my favorite writing skill!*

The Happiest Vendors on Earth

Your key stakeholders, clients, customers, and colleagues are in great hands. As the guest services lead at Disneyland Resorts (Anaheim, CA), I marketed educational and corporate field trips to theme parks and coordinated events and activities for Make-A-Wish children and their families, diplomats, celebrities, and persons with special needs. While at Disneyland, I led planning sessions, brainstorming, and focus groups to spearhead Disney University—Anaheim (member of the first graduating class) and the Disney YES! Program educating youth. *Ask me about the most creative report I have ever presented!*

As your new Program Analyst, I hope to exceed your expectations by successfully completing projects in scope, on time, and under budget. I would love to schedule a time to meet with you and your team in person to discuss your vision for the position. I will follow up with you next week to see if we can meet.

Sincerely,
William Wilberforce

Internship Cover Letter

Go ahead! Be creative. Don't let your life goals be stunted by a stale, plastic cover letter. As a student, you're able to "get away" with placing a lot more life and energy into your cover letter. Let the federal HR team know why you want to work for *their* agency in *this* role, and why *you* are the very best candidate they will ever meet. Your cover letter should certainly be professional, polished, and perfectly edited, but it can have some pizzazz too. Try this one on for size:

SAMPLE COVER LETTER #3

Dear Mrs. Jones,

I am excited to apply for the Pathways Summer Student Internship at the US Department of the Interior, Office of the Secretary in Washington, DC. Currently, I am a full-time student at ABC University.

I have a passion for national parks and indigenous species, and I have closely followed the Department of the Interior programs to support parklands, species, and interpretive programs for the public. This past week, I had the pleasure of visiting the new national park—Kaelia Pond Interpretive Center in Maui, Hawaii. Kaelia is most famous for managing the indigenous species of pink leg birds and the coots. After reviewing the interpretive signs in the building, I drove to the ponds to see the birds in their natural habitat. The park ranger claimed that there were nearly 1,500 pink leg birds in the pond; however, I could only find six birds in total. The water is disappearing at Kaelia, and I would like to study these rare birds and their disappearing home in greater detail to find out why.

Another element of surprise was the lack of visitors in the park that day. The park ranger told me that she was hired to increase community interest in the pond, the pink leg birds, and the new facility. The tiny street sign on the main road did not appear to be doing the trick. It will be fascinating to witness in the future how Kaelia Pond will meet these challenges: funding, lack of water, dwindling bird population, community interest, facility costs, and staff motivation.

For me, the Department of the Interior is just a short Marc train ride from my home in Baltimore. It is my hope that the Office of the Secretary will appreciate my clerical, administrative, computer, communications, scheduling, and research skills for this role and that you will find me to be an environmental advocate and valuable member for the Department of Interior team.

Thank you for your time and consideration. I will follow up with you next week to see if you have any questions regarding my application materials.

Sincerely,
Thomas Clarkson

CHAPTER 9

The Interrogation!
(or the Federal Interview)

Accomplishment will prove to be a journey, not a destination.
—Dwight D. Eisenhower

Congratulations! You have been contacted for an interview, which is no small feat. The federal interview is highly competitive; you must stand out from the competition if you are to land a job offer. We are going to help you do just that.

The type of job seeker you are introduces what type of employee you will become. People who are late for job interviews do not get job offers. Small things add up to make the difference between the candidate who is selected and the others. To be number one and land the job offer, keep in mind that you are being judged …

- *From twelve feet away.* Be kind to the janitor, the scheduler, the secretary, and the security guard. You never know who has influence with friends in high places.
- *From twelve inches away.* Be firm and confident with your handshake.
- *By your first twelve words.* Be communicative and smile.

The federal interview is a two-way communication test. In some overt or covert way, you will be scored, and the interviewee with the highest scores "wins" the job offer. The interview is held to confirm the information on your résumé and the technical skills you claim to have. It is also a test of your personality to ensure it will be a good fit at the agency. You, as the interviewee, are also scoping out the environment and the managers to get a better understanding of how things operate. It is an opportunity for you to get a handle on the job requirements and to better understand the interviewers' personalities and expectations regarding the potential employment opportunity.

Your interview can take the form of a telephone interview, a Skype (or equivalent) interview, or an in-person interview, and you may need to participate in several rounds of interviews. Regardless of the method and frequency, you will most likely meet with a panel of interviewers, usually from three interviewers to up to six or more. Typically, federal hiring managers will select somewhere between three and ten or more highly qualified candidates to interview.

The telephone/Skype interview is your big shot at a tryout in the big leagues, but you have to prove your worth. Treat this opportunity with the same preparation and professionalism that you would for a formal, in-person interview. Print out your résumé, notes, and the vacancy announcement to keep in front of you for personal reference, but do not "read from a script." Make sure that your phone is charged (use a landline if possible) and that you are in a quiet, distraction-free environment. Dress comfortably but professionally (especially for Skype), speak slowly and clearly, and smile while you talk. This will help your positive energy shine through. Do ask about next steps—and do not forget to send a thank-you note via e-mail.

The panel interview or group interview is usually made up of multiple interviewers who are somehow related to your pending position (supervisor, department leaders, colleagues, human resources representatives, etc.). You will either be asked questions by all of these subject matter experts or you will be addressed by one designated officiator while the other selection committee members watch and take notes. Bring multiple copies of your résumé to these interviews and try to sit in a location that allows you to make eye contact with each interviewer.

Accept the last date and time available for your interview. You will want to be the last candidate to interview for the position so that you are the candidate they remember. Sometimes the interview panel will interview ten or fifteen candidates. Leave them with a lasting impression.

BE PREPARED

Research! Research! Research! You want to wow that interview panel. You want to impress them with your vast knowledge of the organization and of the individuals. Ask the point of contact who invited you to interview who you will be interviewing with so you can learn about them and the projects in which they are engaged. Ask questions related to your research findings during the interview. For example, say, "Mr. Tran, I saw on LinkedIn.com that you've been with the Department of ABC for the past ten years. What do you like best about working here?" or "Mr. Hernandez, I saw on the agency website that you were involved with disaster recovery after that devastating tornado in Kansas last summer. What was most challenging for you?" Go to the agency website and analyze several articles, press releases, and project updates to help build a solid knowledge base of the agency's mission and direction. Review the mission statement and strategic-planning documents, and look at the organizational structure (who's in charge and who reports to whom?). Is there a recent piece of legislation that directly affects the organization? Memorizing the history of a federal agency won't hurt your chances either! You can even start to follow the agency on social media like Twitter, Facebook, and LinkedIn. Little things, like knowing the main agency locations or quoting the department secretary, will make you look like the pro that you are. Lastly, review your résumé so you know how to talk intelligently about it. Don't leave any stone unturned when it comes to physically and mentally preparing for your big day.

Tell Me About Yourself (The Elevator Speech)

This question seems informal in nature, but this is not the place to discuss your knitting hobby, favorite reality TV shows, or your child's soccer tournament. The concept behind an elevator speech is for job seekers or career professionals to be able to introduce themselves, their profession, and their career goals in one tiny verbal package that can be revealed in the short span of time that it takes to travel up a few floors on an elevator. This means that if you happen to be in an elevator with a secretary, manager, or diplomat, you have the chance to make a quick and powerful first impression. Use this opportunity to highlight your knowledge, skills, and abilities. This speech can be recycled and reused for job fairs and other networking events. Practice your elevator speech as much as possible—in as many situations as possible. "Pitch" to your spouse, a friend, a parent, the secretary scheduling the interview, the barista making your coffee, and anyone you may meet on the elevator! Below is an example:

My name is Roger Ellis. I am an IT Help Desk professional with more than ten years of experience passionately providing customer service to employees. I have worked as a contractor for three companies, and currently, I am responsible for providing service to over one thousand Department of Transportation employees, both in person and via the telephone. I bring creativity and a collaborative approach to solving the challenges of my customers. Currently, I am attending George Mason University—and majoring in IT systems—to help me further my career goals. I'm excited to be here today to discuss the IT help-desk manager position with your agency.

Interviewers will generally ask you to respond to behavior-based interview (BBI) questions. These are questions that explore your past behavior in a certain situation in an effort to gauge your future behavior in a similar situation. It is a very reliable predictor of how you might behave if they were to select you for the position. One of the best ways to make a great impression is to respond to interview questions with examples. "For example" should be your new favorite phrase for responding, and for goodness sake, use the STAR format (see chapter 5).

Center your interview answers on the value you will bring and highlight the skills you have that will help you exceed expectations in this role. Make sure that every question you answer—even the friendly questions—can "circle back" to your qualifications for this precise career opportunity. You will need to know which attributes are your best and which STAR stories demonstrate them. Use the STAR stories that most closely relate to the job for which you are interviewing. Of course, always radiate positive energy and exude confidence when you respond.

CAREER CLUE

In order to stand out from the competition, practice in front of a mirror and with a digital recorder to hear what you sound like and see what you look like (facial expressions). Your brain will start making pathways to respond in a certain way. The more you practice, the more established these pathways will become. When you enter into a stressful interview environment, your brain will take over, and you will know what to say and how you want to say it. So, practice, practice, practice!

The structure of the federal interview is akin to a formal letter. There is an opening, a body, and a closing. The opening is when you and the interviewers build rapport. Usually a lead interviewer will ask some basic or warm-up questions that will help everyone get on the same page. The opening is the time for you to start building rapport and to answer the initial questions in a way that shows the interview panel that you are serious about the opportunity. They may give you an introduction to the organization or ask what you already know about them.

The transition to the body of the interview will generally be "tell me about yourself." This is where your "elevator pitch" or "thirty-second commercial" is critical. If you ace this question, it can lead to great things during the remainder of the interview. If you bomb this question, it usually goes downhill from here. So make sure you know how you will respond to the "tell me about yourself" question. The closing is where you get to "seal the deal." Oftentimes, interviewers will ask if you have any questions and/or ask why they should hire you. We recommend developing two or three questions and having several reasons why they should hire you at the tip of your tongue.

OUR FAVORITE INTERVIEW PANEL QUESTIONS
- If selected, what would be your priorities for me in the first three months?
- What has been your biggest challenge in the last year?
- What will your organization look like (or what may be different) in one year?
- What does a typical day look like?
- What is the organizational culture?

Bring a solid color two-pocket file folder for each individual on the panel. This file folder can include many different documents (résumé, accomplishment list, awards, publications, letters of recommendation, or references list). The reason for the success portfolio is simple—you are doing something that no other candidate will probably do. It matters very little which documents are included in the file folder or how many you include (three to five is probably best); what matters most is that you are setting yourself apart from the competition. Make sure you have enough copies for each member of the interview panel. You will never regret having extra copies of your documents. Proper preparation makes you look like the pro you are.

Plan to arrive one hour early. These aren't just any hiring managers—and this is not your average interview. If you are entering a federal government facility, there will most likely be challenges that could include commuting (weather and accidents could be factors), parking, guest badging, and security measures—and these are before you enter into the interview location. Mapping out your course the day before (or making a trial run) and giving yourself plenty of time will allow you to be familiar with your route, and you might even have a little wiggle room to "freshen up" and prepare your thoughts before you enter the interview. This hour safety net helps you present yourself as the cool, calm, and polished professional that you are. Find a coffee shop if you are too early. Finally, arrive to your interview location about fifteen minutes before your interview start time.

Not to make you paranoid, but you will be watched! From the second you enter the federal facility to the moment you leave, people are assessing your presence and actions. The people you will come in contact with will create a single judgment about your appearance in just a few seconds! You will want to wear the classiest and most comfortable suit you have in your closet. Try it on if you haven't done so in a while. Men should wear a tailored suit with matching button-front shirt and tie. Aim for a neutral palette, such as black, gray, or navy blue. Pops of color on a silk blouse or power tie are okay—but stay away from busy patterns. Wear shoes that are clean, comfortable, and professional. Be wary of high heels, especially if you aren't used to wearing them. Clothes and shoes that have been worn before and have proven to be comfortable are best. Keep jewelry on the conservative and classy side (think Jacqueline Kennedy), and avoid anything with too much dangle or bling. Make sure that any skirts are knee length or longer and that any blouse is not opaque or see through (you can perform a fluorescent light test to be sure). Do not reveal your back, midriff, or cleavage (men too!), and be certain that no undergarments are showing in any way. Don't forget to cover up tattoos and piercings and make sure your hair is all one "natural" color (the US government isn't that progressive—yet!). Wash up, shave, and wear deodorant, but skip heavy perfumes and colognes. Brush your teeth—twice—and pop in a breath mint on your journey to your interview.

Body language is important. It's a shame that they don't teach us these life skills in school, but body language is a key factor in presenting yourself as a strong, confident professional job candidate. Wait for the interviewer to offer you a seat, and when you take that seat, be ready for the magic to happen. Imagine it is a meeting with your boss for your annual review. In other words, act like you have already gotten the job! Be conscious to not appear shy or arrogant. Smile and perfect your posture by sitting upright and appearing alert and interested. Do not fiddle, bite your nails, crack your knuckles, tap your legs, or twirl your hair around your finger. Be careful to avoid folding your hands, arms, or legs since you do not want to appear closed off. Don't forget to breathe!

TYPICAL FEDERAL INTERVIEW QUESTIONS

Here are a few questions that are common to the federal interview. Learn how to use the STAR format like a pro to ace your federal interview (see chapter 5).

Describe a time or a situation when you ...

- were faced with a stressful situation
- used good judgment in solving a problem
- showed initiative to contain costs
- motivated others (team or direct reports)
- effectively handled a difficult customer
- tried to accomplish something and failed

What is your greatest weakness (area of improvement)?
You always know that this question is coming, but you still cringe when you hear it. The best way to package your answer to this question is to:

- identify a weakness
- tell how you've improved on it
- find a way to turn that weakness into a strength

Here is a good example for those of us with a fear of public speaking:

> I used to be petrified of public speaking, and I would say that this has been my greatest weakness. At my previous position, I was able to join a Toastmasters chapter, and they have really helped me improve upon my public speaking skills. Plus, I was able to network with a lot of wonderful professionals in my field!

If a question stumps you, it is okay to ask for clarity, context, or a few more seconds to think about your response. If you don't know the answer, do not panic. Let the team know that you are not familiar with the term or system they are discussing, but that you will make it a point to learn more about it as soon as possible. Try something like this:

> I have not had personal experience working with that particular software, but I do have five years of experience with a similar software program. I would love to learn more about this new program and would look forward to the opportunity to work with it.

Here is another possible response:

> I have had exposure to database XYZ, but I do not have direct work experience with database XYZ. I am a quick learner, and I taught myself MS Access when no one in my office knew how to use it.

POSTINTERVIEW

Send a thank-you note by e-mail to each panel member who interviewed you within twenty-four hours after the interview (sooner if possible). If you can personalize your message to include something about the interview, that is the best-case scenario. If you do not know their e-mail addresses, send an e-mail to the point of contact who invited you to the interview and ask him or her to forward your thank-you e-mail to the interview panel members. Remember, the type of job seeker you are shows them what type of employee you will become. You want them to know you can complete the mission.

SAMPLE THANK-YOU LETTER

Dear Mr. Sweatt:

Thank you for taking the time to meet with me yesterday to discuss your goals and expectations for the public affairs specialist position at the Department of Agriculture. It was a pleasure to meet with you and your team, and I truly enjoyed learning more about the role and your organization. After our interview, I am confident that my ten years of public affairs experience are a great match for this opportunity, and I believe that I could quickly become a valuable asset on your team.

I am very excited about the possibility of a career with your organization and would be honored to move forward in the hiring process. If you would like any further information, please do not hesitate to contact me at AbrahamLincoln@gmail.com or by phone at 202-202-2222.

Thank you for your time and consideration.

Sincerely,
Abraham Lincoln

FEDERAL INTERVIEW CHECKLIST

	Before the Interview
	Determine the interview logistics (time, location, and type of interview).
	Call or e-mail your references to let them know that you are interviewing for a new position.
	Ask who will be interviewing you/who is on the interview panel.
	Try on and prepare (dry clean/iron/mend) your most comfortable suit and shoes.
	Plan out a professional hairstyle with natural coloring, or treat yourself to a new haircut.
	Map your commute with travel times and print directions (don't simply relay on your smartphone).
	Create a success portfolio.
	Bring a notebook, two (or more) pens, and business cards with you in a briefcase or travel folder. (Did you know the number-one thing an interviewee forgets to bring to an interview is a pen?)
	Research your interviewers (and their careers) via the agency website or LinkedIn.
	Practice your interview questions and elevator speech with friends and family.
	Interview Day
	Skip the perfume and cologne, but make sure to shower, shave, and apply deodorant.
	Conservatively style your hair.
	Dress professionally.
	Arrive in the area at least one hour before your scheduled interview. Plan to arrive at the interview about fifteen minutes beforehand, keeping in mind the security process may be lengthy.
	Turn your phone completely off (vibrate mode can be just as disruptive as a ringtone).
	Throw out any gum or mints, and be careful not to bite your nails or crack your knuckles.
	Greet people by last name, "Mr./Ms. Jones."
	Shake hands—maintain eye contact while providing a firm handshake.
	Accept water if it is offered, but skip the mints, candy, or snacks.
	Smile!
	Make appropriate eye contact with each interviewer.
	Exchange business cards with your interviewer(s), so you can later send a thank-you e-mail.
	After the Interview
	Take notes on what went well and how you can improve for your next interview.
	Send a thank-you note by e-mail to each panel member.
	Take note of any questions you want answered during the next interview (if you have one).

For the Differently Abled

In matters of style, swim with the current; in
matters of principle, stand like a rock.
—Thomas Jefferson

In the US, our country not only accepts different abilities—we celebrate them! We are the nation that raised Stevie Wonder and Helen Keller. Our doctors, scientists, and engineers have transformed the medical field of rehabilitation—restoring movement, sight, hearing, thought, and life to the severely disabled. Even our politicians have put their money where their mouths are on this matter—making reasonable accommodation the law of the land. Persons with disabilities may apply for federal positions noncompetitively (foregoing the more rigorous competitive process).

Federal agencies can fill jobs competitively and noncompetitively. Persons with disabilities may apply for jobs either way. People who are selected for jobs must meet the qualification requirements for the jobs and be able to perform the essential duties of the jobs with or without reasonable accommodation.

Jobs Filled Competitively
Jobs that are filled competitively are advertised through the USAJOBS website. Each job advertisement contains instructions for how to apply.

Jobs Filled Noncompetitively
People with mental retardation, severe physical disabilities, or psychiatric disabilities and have documentation from a licensed medical professional may apply for

noncompetitive appointment through the schedule A (5 C.F.R. 213.3102(u)) hiring authority.

Disabilities may include, but are not limited to, the following:

- blindness
- deafness
- paralysis
- sleep apnea
- epilepsy
- ADHD
- dwarfism
- post-traumatic stress disorder (PTSD)

Official proof-of-disability documentation sources include the following:

- medical doctor
- licensed medical professional
- licensed rehabilitation professional
- agency verification: federal/state/District of Columbia, or US territory
- proof of disability benefits: federal/state/District of Columbia, or US territory
- government-sponsored veterans organization (Veterans Administration)

A sample letter from one of the individuals listed above may look like this:

(Must be on physician's or professional organization's letterhead)

Date

To Whom It May Concern:

This letter serves as certification that Jane Doe is an individual with a documented disability and can be considered for employment under the schedule A hiring authority 5 CFR 213.3102 (u) for people with intellectual disabilities, severe physical disabilities, or psychiatric disabilities.

Thank you for your interest in considering this individual for employment.

You may contact me at (contact information).

Sincerely,
Dr. Edward Hope

US FUN FACT

President Franklin Delano Roosevelt contracted polio as a child and was confined to a wheelchair in his later years. He grew up to be the governor of New York and the president of the United States—elected to a record-breaking four consecutive terms. In WW II, he commanded the lion's share of Allied Force movement from a wheelchair.

In addition to having the Federal Job Results team beside you 100 percent of the way, you have an inside connection when applying. Your secret agent is your *selective placement program coordinator* (SPCC). The SPPC is your agency point of contact who helps recruit, hire, and accommodate persons with disabilities. You can find your SPPC on the OPM website. Applicants should send a federal résumé plus the pertinent documentation (schedule A letter) to the SPPC when communicating. You may wish to connect with the SPPC by e-mail. Below is a sample letter:

Dear placement coordinator,

I would like to be considered for program analyst, GS-13, announcement #FAAJOB123. My online application has been completed in USAJOBS.

I have been with FAA as a contractor for more than five years. I feel that I have a lot of value to bring to the FAA as a direct employee. Over the past several years, I have been directly involved in the flight services organization and a brief time with the aeronautical information management organization before my contract ended while employed with TASC Inc. under the TAC2 contract.

Please inform me of the next steps.

Respectfully,
John Roberts
(703) 555-1212

CAREER CLUE

Make fast friends with your SPPC! Each agency has one (or more) point of contact whose responsibility it is to assist those with disabilities in finding federal government employment. Reach out to him/her to find out what skills are sought and what jobs need filling.

in *PS—Connect with the SPPC on LinkedIn!*

There are dozens of fabulous service organizations that are ready and excited to help you land your dream job. The following are just a few of the government-sponsored or government-affiliated organizations that can provide you with (free) top-notch career search tools:

RESOURCES
Advocacy Organizations
American Association of People with Disabilities
American Council of the Blind
Deaf and Hard of Hearing in Government
Federal Employees with Disabilities
National Council on Independent Living

CHAPTER 11

For Veterans

Our debt to the heroic men and valiant women in the service to our country can never be repaid. They have earned our undying gratitude. America will never forget their sacrifices.
—Harry Truman

Each year, the US Department of Veterans Affairs (VA) hosts a nationwide creative arts competition as one of the many forms of rehabilitative treatment organized to help veterans recover from and cope with physical and emotional injuries. This is no ordinary small-town art show. Like most military strategies, this is a "go big or go home" competition. With fifty-three categories in the visual arts division—ranging from oil painting and sketches to leatherwork and paint-by-number kits—this event is quite the undertaking, requiring an incredible number of participants, workers, and volunteers. In addition, 120 categories promote the performing arts in the areas of dance, music, drama, and creative writing. First-, second-, and third-place awards are nominated in each category by a national selection committee. The winning artists are invited to attend the National Veterans Creative Arts Festival each year.

US FUN FACT

Of the 21.8 million military veterans living in the US today, 1.6 million are women. There are 2.1 million living World War II veterans, 2.6 million Korean War veterans, 7.6 million Vietnam-era veterans, and 4.8 million Gulf War veterans. Five and a half million veterans served in times of peace.

The brave men and women of our US Armed Forces bring valuable knowledge experience and leadership to the federal (and private sector) workforce. Veterans and persons wishing to work with members of our armed services can help serve their government in a number of career fields.

VETERANS' PREFERENCE

Veterans' Preference consists of giving qualified, eligible veterans an advantage over other qualified candidates in the competitive hiring process. Veterans receive hiring preference because of qualifying service or service-connected disability during active duty. Certain veterans can receive Veterans' Preference through qualifying service, service-connected injury or disability, or Purple Heart (awarded for sustaining wounds in action). Spouses, widows, widowers, and mothers of deceased or disabled veterans may also be considered eligible.

Two authorities worth mentioning are the Veterans' Recruitment Appointment (VRA) and the Veterans Employment Opportunity Act of 1998, as amended (VEOA). VRA is an excepted authority that allows agencies, to appoint eligible veterans without competition. You can be appointed under this authority at any grade level up to and including a GS-11 or equivalent. This is an excepted service appointment. After successfully completing two years, you will be converted to the competitive service.

VEOA is a competitive service appointing authority that can only be used when filling permanent, competitive service positions. It cannot be used to fill excepted service positions. It allows veterans to apply to announcements that are only open to so called "status" candidates, which means "current competitive service employees." For additional information visit the FedHireVets.gov website.

THE RATING SYSTEM

You are a five-point-preference eligible if your active duty service meets any of the following:

- 180 or more consecutive days, any part of which occurred during the period beginning September 11, 2001, and ending on a future date prescribed by presidential proclamation or law as the last date of Operation Iraqi Freedom
- between August 2, 1990, and January 2, 1992
- 180 or more consecutive days, any part of which occurred after January 31, 1955, and before October 15, 1976
- in a war, campaign, or expedition for which a campaign badge has been authorized or between April 28, 1952, and July 1, 1955

You are a ten-point-preference eligible if you served at any time and you have

- a service-connected disability or
- a Purple Heart.

Preference-eligible applicants are divided into four basic groups:

- CPS: Disability rating of 30 percent or more (10 points)
- CP: Disability rating of at least 10 percent but less than 30 percent (10 points)
- XP: Disability rating less than 10 percent (10 points)
- TP: Preference-eligible applicants with no disability rating (5 points)

Disabled veterans receive ten points regardless of their disability rating.

Depending on the evaluation method used, agencies determine the best-qualified applicants for a position using a numerical rating and ranking system. Agencies using a numerical rating and ranking system will add an additional five or ten points to the numerical score of qualified preference-eligible veterans. When an agency does not use a numerical rating system, preference-eligible applicants who have a compensable service-connected disability of 10 percent or more (CPS, CP) are placed at the top of the highest category on the referral list (except for scientific or professional positions at the GS-9 level or higher). XP and TP preference-eligible applicants are placed above nonpreference-eligible applicants within their assigned categories.

DOCUMENTATION

For those still on active duty, you can start working for the federal government as soon as you start your terminal leave. Some agencies will not consider your application until you are 120 days out. Others may overlook that if you have a skill set for which they are searching. A federal agency can hold a job opening for you. However, you may run into budget issues (program-funding issues resulting in not filling the vacancy) or management deciding it's not necessary to fill your slot after all if it has taken the hiring manager such a long time to do so—so be careful!

If you are still on active duty, you can get a statement of service from the personnel office or "working" DD-214—written documentation that certifies you are expected to be released from active-duty service under honorable conditions. If you are separating from the military with a 30 percent or more service-connected disability, you will need a letter of rating from the US Department of Veterans Affairs (VA) and a standard form (SF)-15 that will need to be attached to your applications. Please note that it can take a long time (anywhere from a few to eighteen months) to receive your VA letter of rating, but you can start this process prior to separation so you can receive this document sooner. Additionally, you will need to submit the Defense of Department Form 214 (DD-214) to show your military background.

There are multiple organizations that are ready and excited to help you land your dream job. Veterans, there are multiple organizations that are ready and excited to help you land your dream job such as the US Department of Veterans Affairs and the US Department of Labor.

For Students and Recent Graduates

When we study together, we learn together, we
work together and we prosper together.
　　　—Barack Obama

If you are a student or recent graduate, regardless of your age (22 or 122 works!),
one of the easiest ways for you to enter into entry-level federal employment is
through the Pathways Programs. The Pathways Programs offer clear paths to federal
internships for students from high school through postgraduate school and careers
for recent graduates, and they provide meaningful training and career-development
opportunities for individuals who are starting federal service. As a student or recent
graduate, you can begin your career in the federal government by choosing the path
that best describes you and where you are in your academics.

INTERNSHIP PROGRAM

This program is for current students enrolled in a wide variety of educational
institutions—from high school to graduate level—with paid opportunities to work
in agencies and explore federal careers while still in school.

Eligibility
Current students in an accredited high school, college (including four-year colleges/
universities, community colleges, and junior colleges), professional, technical,
vocational, and trade schools, advanced degree programs, or other qualifying

educational institution pursuing a qualifying degree or certificate. Visit the Department of Education's website for a list of acceptable postsecondary institutions and programs.

Program Administration

The internship program is primarily administered by each hiring agency. Agencies may hire interns on a temporary basis for up to one year for an initial period—or for an indefinite period to complete the educational requirement. Interns may work either part-time or full-time. Each agency must sign a participant agreement with the intern that sets forth the expectations for the internship. The intern's job will be related to the intern's academic career goals or field of study. Agencies may provide OPM with information regarding internship opportunities and post information publicly on the USAJOBS website regarding application procedures for specific positions, but they will most likely post them on their local agency websites.

Program Completion and Conversion

Interns may be converted to permanent positions (or, in some limited circumstances, to a term position lasting one to four years) within 120 days of successful completion of the program. To be eligible for conversion, interns must:

- complete at least 640 hours of work experience acquired through the internship program
- complete degree or certificate requirements
- meet the qualification standards for the position to which the intern will be converted
- meet agency-specific requirements as specified in the participant's agreement
- perform the job successfully

Agencies may waive up to 320 of the required 640 hours of work for interns who demonstrate high potential as evidenced by outstanding academic achievement and exceptional job performance. In addition, students working in agencies through third-party intern providers may count up to 320 of the hours they work toward the 640-hour requirement. Time spent under previous internship program appointments may count toward required work-experience hours.

RECENT GRADUATES PROGRAM

This program is for individuals who have recently graduated from qualifying educational institutions or programs (visit the Department of Education's website for a list of acceptable postsecondary institutions and programs) and seek a dynamic career development program with training and mentorship. To be eligible, applicants must apply within two years of degree or certificate completion (except for veterans, precluded from doing so because of their military service obligation, who will have up to six years to apply).

Eligibility

Recent graduates who have completed, within the previous two years, a qualifying associate's, bachelor's, master's, professional, doctorate, vocational or technical degree, or certificate from a qualifying educational institution.

Program Administration

The Recent Graduates Program is administered primarily by each hiring agency. Each agency must sign a participant agreement with the recent graduate that sets forth the expectations for the program. Agencies may provide OPM with information regarding opportunities and post information publicly on the USAJOBS website about how to apply for specific positions.

Training and Development

Participants receive mentorship throughout the program. Individual development plans are developed to track recent graduates' career planning, professional development, and training activities. Participants receive at least forty hours of formal, interactive training each year of the program, and positions offer opportunities for career advancement.

After Program Completion

Recent graduates may be converted to permanent positions (or, in some limited circumstances, a term appointment lasting one to four years). To be eligible for conversion, recent graduates must have:

- successfully completed at least one year of continuous service in addition to all requirements of the program
- demonstrated successful job performance
- met the qualifications for the position to which the recent graduate will be converted

PRESIDENTIAL MANAGEMENT FELLOWS (PMF) PROGRAM

For more than three decades, the PMF program has been the federal government's premier leadership development program for advanced degree candidates.

Eligibility

Individuals who have completed within the past two years, a qualifying advanced degree (e.g., master's or professional degree) or who will meet advanced degree requirements by August 31 of the year following the annual application announcement. An individual may apply for the PMF program more than once as long as he or she meets the eligibility criteria. However, if an individual becomes a finalist and subsequently applies for the PMF program during the next open announcement, the individual will forfeit his or her status as a finalist.

Program Administration

The PMF program is centrally administered by the PMF Program Office within OPM. OPM announces the opportunity to apply for the PMF program (usually in the late summer or early fall) on the USAJOBS website. Applicants go through a rigorous assessment process to determine finalists. OPM selects finalists based on an evaluation of each candidate's experience and accomplishments according to his or her application and results of the assessments. OPM publishes and provides agencies with the list of finalists. Agencies provide OPM with information about their PMF opportunities and can post PMF appointment opportunities for those who are finalists on the PMF website year-round. In addition, a job fair is typically held for finalists each year. Finalists who obtain an appointment as a PMF serve in a two-year excepted service position.

Training and Development

The PMF Program office provides newly hired PMFs an opportunity to receive senior-level mentorship throughout the program. They are also assigned to developmental opportunities in the occupation or functional discipline the PMF would most likely be placed. Participants receive at least eighty hours of formal, interactive training each year of the program, for a total of 160 hours. PMFs are placed on a performance plan and must obtain a successful rating each year.

After Program Completion

After successful program completion and job performance, the PMF may be converted to a permanent position (or, in some limited circumstances, a term appointment lasting one to four years) in the competitive service.

When you submit your federal application package for Pathways opportunities, you will need to prepare a federal résumé. We recommend including a dynamic cover letter to help you stand out from the competition (see chapter 8). For more information on the Pathways programs, visit the USAJOBS website.

Aspiring for the Senior Executive Service (SES)

If your actions inspire others to dream more, learn more,
do more, and become more, you are a leader.
—John Quincy Adams

The Senior Executive Service (SES) leads America's workforce. As the keystone of the Civil Service Reform Act of 1978, the SES was established to provide executive management, ensuring that the US is responsive to its citizens. These leaders possess well-honed executive skills and share a broad perspective on government and a public service commitment that is grounded in the Constitution. Members of the SES serve in the key positions just below the top presidential appointees. SES members are the major link between these appointees and the rest of the federal workforce. They operate and oversee nearly every government activity in approximately seventy-five federal agencies. OPM manages the overall SES program, providing approval of candidates and oversight of program activities as agencies implement their programs.

There are usually three options for applying, but the applicant must apply as required in the "How to Apply" section of the vacancy announcement:

Traditional ECQ Narrative Method
Using this method, the vacancy announcement directs applicants to submit an SES résumé and narratives addressing the Executive Core Qualifications (ECQs) and any technical qualifications. The ECQ statement, addressing all five ECQs, is limited to a

maximum of ten pages. OPM has a specific format for the traditional method, and it needs to be adhered to exactly as stated.

Each ECQ should have one or two examples—we recommend two. The first example needs to be about three-quarters of the response and very strong (with significant detail), and the other makes up the last one-fourth of the response. Of course, if you have two equally strong examples, use both—but make sure you remain under two pages in total.

Most important is that the examples show depth and breadth of leadership experience. Each example within the ECQ needs to reflect the context, challenge, action, result (C-C-A-R) structure. Actually typing these words into your document as you draft it can be helpful for ensuring you are addressing these concepts; you can delete them later. You need to make sure the ECQ "proves" competencies (see below) using work history going back no further than ten years. It generally takes an average of twenty hours to prepare a complete set of ECQs using this method.

Résumé Only

This option was designed primarily for high-level positions requiring sophisticated leadership skills or positions with hard-to-obtain technical qualifications that will likely limit the number of applicants. Under this method, the vacancy announcement directs applicants to submit only a federal résumé. Applicants show possession of the ECQs and any technical qualifications via the résumé. Agencies generally limit résumés to no more than five pages, including an optional cover letter (see chapters 6 and 8). It generally takes an average of ten hours to prepare an ECQ résumé.

Accomplishment Record

Under this method, the vacancy announcement directs applicants to submit a résumé and narratives addressing selected competencies (e.g., strategic thinking) underlying the ECQs and any technical qualifications. This permits candidates to submit a more streamlined application targeting the selected competencies instead of the lengthy ECQ narratives that have become standard. Agencies generally identify five competencies—one for each ECQ—that applicants must address in accordance with the instructions in the vacancy announcement. Narratives addressing the competencies are normally limited to one page per competency. It generally takes an average of fifteen hours to prepare a complete set of ECQs using this method.

ECQ COMPETENCIES

Below is a list of the competencies:

ECQ 1 Leading Change

This core qualification involves the ability to bring about strategic change, both within and outside the organization, to meet organizational goals. Inherent to this ECQ is the ability to establish an organizational vision and to implement it in a continuously changing environment.

Competencies

- creativity and innovation
- external awareness
- flexibility
- resilience
- strategic thinking
- vision

ECQ 2 Leading People

This core qualification involves the ability to lead people toward meeting the organization's vision, mission, and goals. Inherent to this ECQ is the ability to provide an inclusive workplace that fosters the development of others, facilitates cooperation and teamwork, and supports constructive resolution of conflicts.

Competencies

- conflict management
- leveraging diversity
- developing others
- team building

ECQ 3 Results Driven

This core qualification involves the ability to meet organizational goals and customer expectations. Inherent to this ECQ is the ability to make decisions that produce high-quality results by applying technical knowledge, analyzing problems, and calculating risks.

Competencies

- accountability
- customer service
- decisiveness
- entrepreneurship
- problem solving

ECQ 4 Business Acumen

This core qualification involves the ability to manage human, financial, and information resources strategically.

Competencies

- financial management
- human capital management
- technology management

ECQ 5 Building Coalitions

This core qualification involves the ability to build coalitions internally and with other federal agencies, state and local governments, nonprofit and private-sector organizations, foreign governments, or international organizations to achieve common goals.

Competencies

- partnering
- political savvy
- influencing/negotiating

The Insider's Guide to Using USAJOBS.gov

When you reach the end of your rope, tie a knot in it and hang on.
—Thomas Jefferson

The USAJOBS website is the US government's official website for listing civil service job opportunities with federal agencies. The site is operated by OPM. It is our recommendation that you use the USAJOBS website as the hub for your federal job search because it keeps an ongoing record of all the applications you submit. When you get your federal interview, you can go back and review the vacancy announcement. You need to start by creating your account profile in the USAJOBS website. Follow these steps to ensure you have a great start in the USAJOBS website system.

CREATE YOUR ACCOUNT PROFILE

To create a USAJOBS account, you will need to select "Create An Account" link located at the top right-hand side of the home page. Fill in all of the required fields on this page pertaining to your personal information.

Submit your information by clicking on the confirmation button at the bottom of the page. If you receive a message stating there is already an account with your e-mail address, you may already have an account. Unfortunately, the USAJOBS website does not allow more than one account per e-mail address. If this occurs, enter a new e-mail address that you have access to and resubmit your information.

I agree. Create my account.

CREATE YOUR RÉSUMÉ

Although it may take you longer to do so, it is strongly recommended that you input your résumé into the system as opposed to uploading it. There are exceptions to this rule, but for the most part, an inputted résumé is best. There are a number of reasons why this is preferred. First, the résumé you build will be able to be accepted by other application systems when needed, whereas an uploaded résumé may not. Second, the résumé builder is designed to ensure that you have provided the standard information required for your federal résumé by prompting you for responses. Uploading your résumé does not ensure that you have included all the required information. Third, the system is designed to help agencies evaluate applications more easily by receiving the required information in a standard and uniform format. In other words, the HR team is familiar with the USAJOBS website résumé builder format.

You can copy and paste information from your résumé into the résumé builder text fields. Please note that there is a limit of five résumés per account. Simply follow these steps to get started:

To create your résumé in the system, you will need to select *My Account> Resumes> Build New Resume.*

Then, go through the steps for inputting your information (experience, education, other, references, preview, and finish). Cut and paste your information into the résumé builder.

When entering your résumé, we recommend the first job listed to be your professional profile. This is one way to enter your information so that your career summary will appear at the top of your résumé. The position title should be "Professional Profile" and the employer should be "Career Summary." Use your personal address to fill in the employer address, and copy and paste your résumé information into the corresponding sections. Below is a visual example of how the professional profile is inputted into the first job entry into the USAJOBS website résumé builder.

Your Federal Résumé

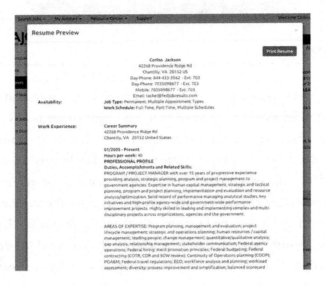

Input your professional profile into the first job entry.

When naming your résumé, you can name it by job title or simply use the current date. Naming it by date will allow you to quickly identify the latest version.

We recommend selecting "Non-Confidential." Selecting "Confidential" will hide your contact information, current employer name, and references from recruiters performing résumé searches. It doesn't happen often, but it certainly can't hurt!

Confidentiality
◯ Confidential ◯ Non-Confidential

- Remember to always save your work!

If Your Duties Exceed the Character Limit

The "Duties, Accomplishments, and Related Skills" section will only allow five thousand characters. If your duties description is more than five thousand characters, please use this work-around:

- Cut and paste as many complete paragraphs in the duties section as will fit. Then, include at the end in parentheses:

"(Continued in Additional Information Section)"

Duties, Accomplishments and Related Skills

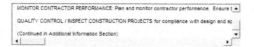

Character Count: 2,772 (5,000 character limit)

- Then, in the "Other" section about halfway down the page, there is a section called "Additional Information," which allows for twenty thousand characters. Input your remaining text into "Additional Information" by starting out with the following phrase, "Continued from Job 2."

Need more space? Expand this field.

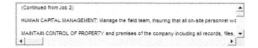

Character Count: 4,216 (20,000 character limit)

- "Additional Information" is also the section for including any information from your résumé that doesn't have a specific place in the résumé builder in which to enter it (i.e., LinkedIn URL, Job-Related Honors, Awards,

Leadership Activities, Computer Skills, Typing Speed, etc.). Remember this section allows for twenty thousand characters.

- Finally, click on "Next" and "Activate your Resume."

CREATE YOUR SEARCH ENGINE

Job search agents help you look for jobs in your area of interest. The agent will automatically search for jobs based on your search criteria and e-mail you when new jobs are entered into the database that meet your specifications. The USAJOBS agent creation, deletion, editing, and viewing functions are all located within "My Account."

To create a search agent, simply follow these instructions:

- Log in to the USAJOBS website.
- Select the "My Account" tab at the top of the page.
- Click on "Saved Searches" on the left. Then select "Create a New Saved Search."
- Specify the search criteria. We recommend specifying "Salary or Pay Grade," "Occupational Series or Job Category," and "Location" initially. You can always add or modify your criteria in the future.
- Scroll down to the bottom of the search and respond to the question: "How often do you want to receive e-mail notifications to your primary e-mail address?" Opt in to receive your search results daily because you might miss out on opportunities if you select weekly or monthly.
- Give your search agent a name and save it.

You can also create a search agent by conducting a job search and selecting the "Save this Search" and "E-Mail Me Jobs" links at the top and bottom of the job search results page.

CAREER CLUE

Create a job-search alert in the USAJOBS website! We suggest a daily notification over a weekly update because a weekly selection may cause you to miss out on a great opportunity.

Security Clearance

It has been my experience that folks who
have no vices have very few virtues.
　　　　—Abraham Lincoln

You have made it past the hardest part of the federal hiring process, which is being recognized as an exceptional candidate, obtaining the coveted interview, and winning the position over your close competition. However, before you are able to walk into your shiny new cubicle, you will need to be properly vetted by the powers that be. The security office in your organization will have established a level of security clearance required to perform your daily duties.

After completing your security paperwork (Form SF-85 or SF-86), your packet will be forwarded to the security department that will assign your case to a series of field background investigators to confirm the accuracy of your background information (education, residences, employment, law checks, military checks, mental health records, and credit checks). The depth and breadth of your background check is contingent upon the position for which you are applying, and the length of your security process will be determined by the level of clearance required.

An official US government security clearance will determine your eligibility for access to classified information, and it is only granted to those for whom an appropriate personnel security background investigation has been completed. Throughout the course of the investigation, it must be determined that your personal and professional history indicates loyalty to the US, strength of character, trustworthiness, honesty, reliability, discretion, and sound judgment. Your investigation should present freedom from conflicting allegiances, patterns of illegal or destructive behaviors, and be void of potential for blackmail or coercion. The collection of law checks, documents, and in-person interviews that make up your security clearance will need to display a certain level of reliability as well as a willingness and ability to abide by the law, follow rules, regulations, and governing authorities while exercising proper care, handling, and protection of classified information.

FILING YOUR SECURITY PACKET

Even with a perfect background and squeaky-clean legal record, the government security paperwork (SF-86/SF-85) can be a very intimidating process. The paperwork alone may take days or weeks to properly complete. The key word in every background check is, in fact, "complete." Any blank left on these official forms is marked as an issue or "flag." It will greatly behoove you—in adjudication (approval rating) and timeliness (start date of your job)—if you correctly list every neighbor, coworker, legal infraction, credit ding, nickname, and employment/military location (TDY included) on your security paperwork. Below is a table that lists the basic security clearance process.

	SECURITY CLEARANCE PROCESS	
1	Complete Security Forms	Complete and submit all security clearance paperwork such as SF-85/SF-86
2	Law Checks	Law checks/fingerprints run for each state where you have lived and worked
3	Record Checks	Records maintained for the following: employment, housing, education (transcript, dean record, campus law), mental health, military records, legal paperwork, and various background records as needed
4	Credit Checks	Pulled from all three credit bureaus—specifically searching for outstanding bills, liens, bankruptcies, foreclosures, and inappropriate use of funds
5	Reference Check	In-person interviews are conducted with neighbors, colleagues, supervisors, neighbors, and classmates. Family members are not used as references.
6	Leads Interviewed	Investigators are required to interview two persons per work, education, and residential location. The investigator must locate leads (references not listed on initial paperwork) to complete reference requirements.
7	Issues	Issues (legal, credit, divorce, firing, etc.) must be followed up with both a record check and in-person interviews from witnesses or colleagues. Previous or current spouses may be interviewed for resolution if necessary.
8	Interview (if applicable)	For top secret interviews (or higher clearance), an in-person interview will take place. You will review your security paperwork and discuss any issues and/or discrepancies. You can clarify "gray areas" with your lead investigator.

SECURITY CLEARANCE PROCESS		
9	Extensions	After the interview, case extensions will be scheduled to obtain additional records, documents, and reference interviews. Extensions are scheduled for developed work sites, education, residential, credit, character, or legal issues.
10	Adjudication	Final reports are filed by field investigators, packaged, and submitted to OPM. After OPM reviews and "adjudicates" your case files, your clearance outcome will be forwarded to your hiring agency (DOD, DOJ, etc.) for final adjudication.

There are several different types of background checks and clearances. Below is a list:

CLEARANCE	REQUIREMENTS
Confidential "Public Trust"	Provides access to information that reasonably could be expected to cause damage to national security if disclosed to unauthorized sources (primarily military). Includes National Agency Check with Local Agency Check and Credit Check (NACLC).
Secret	Provides access to information that could reasonably be expected to cause serious damage to the national security if disclosed to unauthorized sources. Requires an NACLC.
Top Secret	Provides access to national security, counterterrorism, counterintelligence, or other highly sensitive data that could cause exceptionally grave damage to national security if disclosed to unauthorized sources. Requires a Single Scope Background Investigation (SSBI) and may take three to eighteen months to complete.
BI	Bureau of Immigration clearance, specifically used by the US Customs and Border Protection.
NACI	National Agency Check with Inquiries, specifically used by the Department of Justice.
SCI	Sensitive Compartmented Information (SCI) provides information access assigned in "compartments" for a short or extended time so that a person with access to one compartment has no access to others. Examples include cryptography, communications, and nuclear stockpile information.
SAP	Special Access Programs (SAP) provide access to exceptionally vulnerable information, such as stealth technology.
L Clearance	Provides civilian access to nuclear materials and information.
Q Clearance	Provides civilian access to atomic or nuclear-related materials for nonmilitary personnel.
Yankee White	Administrative nickname for a background check for personnel working with the president (Executive Office of the President).

You can save yourself time, stress, and possibly a security clearance by simply reading and following the complete set of directions for each section. For example, if you are applying for a Top Secret Clearance and your SF-86 paperwork is requesting the past ten years of residential locations, do not list eight years of residence or eleven years of residence—list ten.

Your required years of employment, residence, military service, credit, and mental health background will vary by your type of clearance, agency, and whether or not you have been cleared previously for another position. For many individuals who have previously held cleared positions, paperwork may only need to include between three and five years of new information, but rest assured that your paperwork will let you know exactly how many years must be fully covered.

For many individuals, these five-, seven-, or ten-year benchmarks may save you a lot of hassle, such as avoiding a credit issue resulting from that crazy roommate you had in college or that time you were reprimanded at your first fast-food position when you were late because you forgot to set your alarm clock. On a grander scale, some alcohol issues (DUI, possession, etc.), mental health records, and place-of-employment infractions *may* be eliminated from your background simply because they happened before the "scope" (time frame) that is required by your clearance paperwork. Do not add more work for yourself or your investigative security team.

REFERENCES

Please make certain to list full contact information for each person (neighbor, supervisor, coworker, reference), including current phone number, physical address, e-mail address, and location of employment. It is honestly better to wait a couple of days to obtain this updated information than to leave blank sections or outdated information. Blank sections are flagged as issues on background checks, and incorrect/outdated material is flagged as "discrepant" information. Each day that your background investigator spends chasing this information is a day that you will be waiting for your clearance to pass—and your new dream career to start!

If your investigator is unable to contact a reference listed on your paperwork because of outdated information, he or she will need to develop a new lead—one whom you may or may not want your investigator to contact. For example, Supervisor Susie may have found you to be an exemplary employee at Awesome Analysts, Inc.; however, you unfortunately listed an older phone number for her previous project location. Since your investigator was unable to contact your favorite supervisor, the investigator will need to visit your project location to locate new reference leads (they cannot leave this section blank). When visiting your project site, your investigator meets one of your previous coworkers, Johnny Nay-Sayer, and proceeds to interview Johnny about your time as an awesome analyst. Mr. Nay-Sayer is still secretly disgruntled about you receiving that big promotion over him last year and proceeds to paint a not-so-glorious picture of your life and work ethic. Furthermore, Mr. Nay-Sayer proceeds to provide new leads for the investigator to interview, Fiona FacebookTooMuch and Larry Lazy-kins, who were also passed up for the position.

Now, rather than your true top-notch job performance being represented on your security clearance, a new, bleaker image is presented to OPM and your government agency. Now are you ready to locate that updated information? LinkedIn, Facebook, friends and colleagues, and company websites are great ways to quickly track down current and complete contact information for your best references.

CREDIT REPORT

Okay, maybe you have a perfect 800 credit score and have never missed a payment since you bought your first Easy-Bake Oven with your Fisher-Price cash register. For the rest of us, it is important to monitor our credit scores—if only to be proactive against incidents of credit fraud or identity theft.

Having a ding on your credit score does not immediately disqualify you from obtaining a security clearance. However, a significant pattern of bad credit and overall poor money management may hinder or end your clearance prospects. Credit issues, like all issues that may arise within a security clearance, are ranked by the effect they may hold on personal vulnerability and possibility of blackmail or coercion. As far as the government is concerned, a person who owes $150,000 to various collection agencies is more likely to sell military secrets to Russia than a person who owes $150 to a rich uncle. In addition, the type of credit issue present is likely to play a role in the categorization (ranking) of the problem. For example, a person who owes back taxes or has defaulted on federal student loans is considered to have a higher credit incident rate than someone who missed his or her last payment to their Homeowner's Association (HOA). Assess the type of work you are applying for. If you are applying for an accountant position with the federal government or a management opportunity at the IRS, you better make sure you have a stellar credit score (and owe no back taxes!). Please do everything you can to eliminate items on your credit report prior to submitting your clearance paperwork, especially if there are small items you may be able to knock off the list in a short period of time.

For those credit issues that are larger in scale, just make sure that you are taking pivotal steps to eradicate the issue. This means making direct contact to arrange a payment plan. Take note of the date, time, and person contacted when addressing your credit item, as well as documenting the agreement and payment plan. When you attend your security interview (required for some levels), you will have the chance to explain yourself and communicate with your investigator about the positive steps you have made to improve your credit health. That being said, credit issues are the number-one issue disqualifier for federal clearances—so take this matter seriously.

Most people have gotten a speeding ticket, accidentally missed a cell phone payment, or hung out with that one friend with whom they wish they hadn't. Furthermore, many people have had at least one employment or military review that was not up to par, and/or "experimented" in certain "extracurricular activities" while in college. On the topic of marijuana—yes, this is certainly flagged as an issue. Yes, even if you live in a state where it has been legalized for certain uses, this is still flagged as an issue (marijuana is still classified as a Schedule 1 drug by the federal government, regardless of a state ruling). That being said, former drug or alcohol abuse will be labeled as an issue, but it may be assessed as a lower-level issue depending on how many years ago the usage took place, the frequency, and whether or not you are still participating in these activities. Regarding traffic violations, a speeding or parking ticket does not need to be listed. It is only necessary to list a traffic violation if the issue was ultimately classified as a felony (DUI/DWI/Excessive Speeding, etc.), in which case you would address this issue under the question relating to felonies.

Tell the Truth!

Ultimately, it is best to record these issues on your paperwork the first time. A "developed" (not initially reported) issue such as drug abuse or DUI/DWI that is discovered during your clearance process will most likely result in dismissal of your case (and possibly a federal offense). Substance abuse issues are often discovered throughout the course of the investigation by campus law checks, state and federal law checks, and personal interviews with friends, relatives, and colleagues. By stating the steps you have made to eradicate the behavior, you will be painting a bigger picture of your background.

Overall, the government wants to make certain that your actions and behaviors cannot be used against you in terms of blackmail or coercion. Telling the truth the first time will save you time (and possibly your clearance). Many drug/alcohol questions ask you to go back a certain number of years (usually one, three, five, seven, or ten) depending on the level of clearance. You do not need to list/discuss these issues if the use or incident occurred prior to the period of coverage. However, if the question reads, "Have you ever," then you are required to list it.

Make a List and Check It Twice

Residences

Make sure to list all residences within the coverage period with full contact information for a neighbor(s). If you absolutely, positively have never had any contact with neighbors at a certain location, list someone who physically visited your residence (preferably a nonrelative). Having more than one contact is always a good thing.

References

Select people who love you and will brag about your skills and personality—people who will refer your investigator to other people who love you as well. Do not list family members! Listing a family member will only prolong your investigation since your investigator will need to make multiple in-person attempts to develop leads and interview nonrelatives.

Education

List a professor or classmate (with full contact information). Since the education security process includes a campus law check, any infractions you may have received in college will be noted in your investigation.

Employment

Make certain to list both your company/headquarters address as well as your physical work location(s). Listing both addresses on your paperwork will save time on your clearance process and avoid a mark of "discrepancy."

Foreign Travel

You are required to list foreign travel for a certain number of years (not your entire life). Make sure to include countries visited on ports of entry on cruise vacations as well as trips to Canada and Mexico. Military personnel should list stations, TDY locations, and deployments. Follow the instructions; some foreign travel on official government business is not required to be listed. For recent graduates, remember to include study abroad trips.

SECURITY INTERVIEW PREP

Many security clearances will require an in-person security interview to look over your security paperwork, address any issues, fill in gaps in information, and develop new leads. For your interview, you should dress professionally and arrive on time (or early). A best practice would be to bring a notebook, pen, and an updated address book or smartphone with current contact information for friends, neighbors, and colleagues (in case any contact information has changed since you filed your paperwork).

If you have had credit concerns in the past, it would be advantageous to pull a credit report prior to your interview to give you a chance to obtain updated payment plan information that you may be able to share with your investigator to prove you are making all efforts to rectify any issues. Other than that, just relax and answer the questions openly and honestly. The security interview is one of the last steps in your security clearance process, which means they are serious about you.

CHAPTER 16

Social Media

Things may come to those who wait, but only
those things left by those who hustle.
—Abraham Lincoln

Social media is no longer confined to a subset of America's teens and college students.
The US government has harnessed the power of social media to connect with citizens
at home and abroad to easily communicate official information. By leveraging media
tools such as Twitter, Facebook, LinkedIn, and YouTube, the US government is able
to publicize events, rapidly convey messages, and educate the public on important
new policies, procedures, and safety awareness.

It is important to confirm the authentication of each media source to ensure that
it is, in fact, managed by the federal government. You can look up accounts managed
by federal agencies, elected officials, heads of agencies, and members of the president's
cabinet. Many .com, .edu, and .org URLs maintain very helpful information, but all
official federal, state, and tribal government websites are followed by .gov. USA.gov
has a helpful search tool that allows you to verify the authenticity of federal social
media outlets, such as the Official White House Twitter account.

CAREER CLUE

Verifying Federal Government Social Media Accounts: A handy search
tool is present at USA.gov to help verify traditional (and nontraditional)
online media outlets owned and operated by US federal, state, and
tribal governments.

Social Media

While social media may not directly help you land a job, it is important to stay up to date on important issues, events, and policies that directly affect your field of interest or agency of choice. Knowledge of current events, trends, leaders, and power players can give you the upper hand in an interview.

Traditional knowledge tools (newspapers, magazines, and trade journals) and participation in professional organizations also serve as fantastic ways to sharpen your expertise and expand your career network. By closely following movements, research, and development, you will be able to tailor your career, résumé, training, and education toward a subset of state-of-the-art knowledge, skills, and abilities that the average applicant may simply not think to address.

Media Outlets

Official federal government online media outlets include (but are not limited to) Blip, Disqus, Facebook, Flickr, Foursquare, Girhub, Google+, IdeaScale, LinkedIn, Meetup, MySpace, Pinterest, Posterous, Scribd, Slideshare, Socrata, Storify, Tumblr, Twitter, Uservoice, Ustream, Vimeo, and YouTube. You can be certain that the US government will maintain its official (.gov) websites and will continue to stay up to date, innovative, and trendy in the realm of new media.

US FUN FACT

Eleanor Roosevelt was the first first Lady to hold her own press conference in 1933. Her one rule was that only female journalists were permitted to attend. Why? By enforcing this decree, news outlets were forced to hire female journalists at a pivotal moment in the fight for women's suffrage and equal rights.

The Blogosphere

Official government blogs are the news outlets of choice for most federal agencies. Although tools such as Facebook and LinkedIn are also highly exploited, blogs allow an agency to go a bit more in depth about current programs, projects, events, and initiatives. Blogs tend to be longer than e-mails and shorter than essays, and they can serve as quick reads for folks trying to stay on top of what's what and who's who in a certain department or field of interest.

Check out this post by David Hudson discussing the ConnectED initiative shared by both the White House blog (whitehouse.gov/blog) and the Department of Education blog (ed.gov/blog) regarding the future of digital content in the American classroom:

The Federal Communications Commission (FCC) will invest $2 billion over the next 2 years to dramatically expand high-speed Internet connectivity for America's schools and libraries—connecting more than 20 million students to next generation broadband and wireless. In addition, private-sector companies have committed more than $750 million to deliver cutting-edge technologies to classrooms including:

- Apple, which will donate $100 million in iPads, MacBooks, and other products, along with content and professional development tools to enrich learning in disadvantaged US schools
- AT&T, which pledged more than $100 million to give middle school students free Internet connectivity for educational devices over their wireless network for three years
- Autodesk, which pledged to make their 3-D design program "Design the Future" available for free in every secondary school in the US—more than $250 million in value
- Microsoft, which will launch a substantial affordability program open to all US public schools by deeply discounting the price of its Windows operating system, which will decrease the price of Windows-based devices
- O'Reilly Media, which is partnering with Safari Books Online to make more than $100 million in educational content and tools available for free to every school in the US
- Sprint, which will offer free wireless service for up to 50,000 low-income high school students over the next four years, valued at $100 million
- Verizon, which announced a multiyear program to support ConnectED through up to $100 million in cash and in-kind commitments.

Newsflash

By reading this post, you have not only learned about a pretty awesome education initiative, but you have acquired some knowledge about the direction in which certain departments, agencies, and private sector companies are moving.

Finding Inspiration and Motivation for Your Federal Job Search

If your actions inspire others to dream more, learn more,
do more, and become more, you are a leader.
—John Quincy Adams

Motivation is what separates the go-getters from the "maybe laters." Motivation is the difference between getting up in the morning and sleeping in each day. More important, motivation is the key factor in separating the federally hired from the (still-to-be) federally desired. What motivates you? (Feel free to note your selections from chapter 1). Is it patriotism and service to country? Is it access to the latest and greatest technology and programs? Is it adventure and the opportunity for career growth? Maybe you simply desire a solid foundation of job security and benefits for you and your family. These are all incredible motivators. Pick yours and hold on tight because it's going to be a rocky road.

If self-motivation is not your strongest attribute, try to pull inspiration from family, friends, and influential folks in your network. Pack up your car and volunteer for the day—or the week. Remember that every time you wake up an hour early to exercise or cook a healthy breakfast, each minute you spend perfecting your federal résumé instead of lounging on social media, and each time you substitute a TV marathon with a federal career search, you are moving closer to your goal.

If you are still struggling to connect with your higher power, try looking at your favorite American heroes. Think about them. Talk about them. Read their biographies. Reconnect with agencies, organizations, and nonprofits that you care about and those that your heroes would support. Consider the inspirational life story of Chris Kyle (Navy SEAL and veteran volunteer) or astronaut John Glenn's legendary moon walk and subsequent congressional service and professorship. Read (or reread) the works of Maya Angelou, Frederick Douglass, or Rev. Dr. Martin Luther King Jr. Think about former congresswoman and shooting victim Gabrielle Giffords and her political activism on behalf of gun violence victims and their family. Remember 9/11 first responders and the more recent heroism of military servicemen Anthony Sadler, Spencer Stone, and Alek Skarlatos as they overpowered radical terrorists on a train ride in France. None of these Americans came from an influential or wealthy background, yet they each set into motion a trajectory of hope and commitment that has shaped our nation and collective conscience.

You're going to have a lot of excuses. Do not give in.
—Abraham Lincoln

However many excuses you have, Abraham Lincoln had more. Not many folks are aware that the famous US president lost eight elections, failed two businesses, was laid off from multiple jobs, was rejected from law school, and suffered a mental breakdown (like completely-in-bed-for-six-months mental breakdown). He even ran for Congress (1843—lost), reran (1846—won), and was voted back out of office in 1848. Talk about rejection! These are not the typical credentials that you may expect from one of the most influential US presidents.

Now if you think that his professional aspirations were flawed, Abraham Lincoln's home life was even more tragic. Baby Abe was born into poverty on February 12, 1809, inside a one-room log cabin in Hodgenville, Kentucky. His mother died when Abe was just nine years old as the result of milk sickness—a rare disease caused by cows that digest poison plants. Abe's father moved the family to Illinois to attempt a new life—and Abraham was put to work as a child to support the family. Young Abe only had one year of formal education, but he read books ferociously and maintained a constant hunger for learning.

His first love, Ann Rutledge, had been engaged to another and then died miserably of fever shortly after accepting Lincoln's (rumored) proposal of marriage. This event prompted Lincoln to claim he would never use the word *love* again (and is suspected to be at the root of his total breakdown). When he did marry, he had a tumultuous relationship (at best) with Mary Todd. They lost three sons at heartbreakingly young ages (Eddie Lincoln, age four to tuberculosis; Willie Lincoln, age twelve to fever; and

Tad Lincoln, age eighteen to heart failure). His fourth son, Robert Lincoln lived into adulthood. Both Abraham and Mary Todd suffered from constant depression and mental illness as the result of the loss of their beloved children—and have no living descendants.

I don't know about you, but I would have quit somewhere after my second job layoff or rejection from law school. I would have thrown in the towel and signed up for the nearest minimum-wage gig that I could find on the wide-open prairie. But what if Abraham Lincoln had quit? What would America look like if "Good ol' Abe" had not been our president? Would we have a United States or separate war-torn Northern and Southern territories? Would slavery still exist in America? Would persons from other cultures be able to vote or own property if it had not been for the acts created by Mr. Lincoln?

What if Abraham Lincoln had quit? I shudder at the thought.

TEN KEYS TO CRACKING THE CODE

When things aren't going your way or you start to feel like quitting, read these helpful hints below. These are the ten keys to cracking the code that should help you stay on track and reach your goals of obtaining a federal job or furthering your federal career.

Search outside of metropolitan areas.
Look at jobs that are outside of the area where public transportation covers. Search in suburbs and around the exteriors of metropolitan areas. Many job seekers will not apply to jobs in locations where public transportation does not go. Although your commute may not be ideal, once you have survived your probationary period (usually one year), it is a lot easier to move to another position once you are in the system.

Look at temp and term appointments.
These are nonpermanent appointments in which you gain job skills, experience, and valuable networking opportunities. Plus, of course, a paycheck. If and when the job is announced permanently, you can apply (yes, this is required), knowing the hiring managers know you and your work ethic.

Understand the federal qualification requirements.
Federal applications must convey that the applicant already has the skills required to do the job. Many people apply to jobs they could easily do—without having the specific skills. The minimum requirement is that you must have twelve months of experience doing that same or similar work.

Identify the best jobs for your background.

Many people apply to jobs that are not good fits for them. Use a technique we call the "80 percent rule." Carefully review the vacancy announcement language, particularly under the "Duties" tab. Look for an 80 percent match between the duties listed and your skills. This is a great technique to determine if the job in the vacancy announcement is a good fit for you.

Create a federal résumé.

Do not try to apply for a federal government job with a private-sector résumé. It is too short and does not include the information required to score the most points during the rating and ranking process. Make your federal résumé lengthy. The average federal résumé is three to five pages and extremely detailed. A federal résumé addresses your skills and competencies, and a private sector résumé focuses on results and accomplishments—two very different objectives. Many federal application packages focus on accomplishments and do not include the "nitty-gritty" details, which result in the highest possible score. The more detailed the information you provide, the more points your application is likely to score during the rating and ranking process.

Be sure you have the right content in your federal résumé.

Federal résumés need to be extremely detailed and written with descriptive adjectives. Words like *complex* and *routinely* are meaningful to the federal HR specialist.

Answer the self-assessment questions liberally—with fervor.

Most online applications ask applicants to rate their professional experience by using a series of questions. The applicant needs to receive the highest rating in order to move forward in the rating process. Review the answers to the question and select the one that represents the most senior experience level (the one that is worth the most points). Give yourself credit! Do not be dishonest, but boast, brag, market yourself, rationalize, and justify—whatever you want to call it. Make sure your résumé supports your responses. Remember it is called a "self-assessment questionnaire" for a reason!

Include KSAs (knowledge, skill, and ability statements) in your federal résumé.

With hiring reform, HR specialists are looking for the KSAs to be incorporated into the résumé. Since hiring reform changes took effect in 2010, most federal agencies no longer require you to write narrative essays when you initially apply for a job. However, it is totally your responsibility to make sure you possess the required KSAs and incorporate them into your résumé. Otherwise, you will be deemed not qualified for the position because you didn't tell them you have the skills by incorporating the KSAs into your résumé.

Work your network.

Although you have to be able to get through the initial stages of the federal application process on your own, it can help if your application lands in the hands of a hiring manager you've networked with before. How? He or she can select whomever is best qualified—why not you? One savvy method to get a chance to speak with a federal government official is to request an informational interview with a federal employee (preferably a hiring manager). An informational interview (not a job interview) will enable you to learn about the agency and its needs and give you a chance to convey your skills to a federal hiring manager. How do you get an informational interview? Start by asking neighbors, friends, and family members who work or are affiliated with the federal government!

Be persistent!

You have to be persistent and consistent about applying for federal jobs on a regular basis and following up on your applications. It can take dozens (or more) of applications and from three to eighteen months to get a federal interview with a hiring manager. (This is a bureaucracy, after all!). If you are getting results that show you are eligible—not referred—it is still good. It means you are applying to the right jobs for your background, but you might need to improve your application package.

FORWARD STEPS

You may hear from some naysayers—but don't let them dictate your future. You may hear about how your neighbor got a federal job –but every situation is different. By reading this book, you have now equipped yourself with insider knowledge, which can save you a significant amount of both time and energy. Everyone's journey is different and there will be some obstacles along the way. You have taken the first step of preparation by reading this book. Now it is time to take the next few steps toward your dream of obtaining a federal job.

Remember Abraham Lincoln and the rocky road he had to plow to reach his goals and dreams. We are quite certain that his daily commute was uphill both ways—in a Midwest prairie blizzard. "You cannot escape the responsibility of tomorrow by evading it today," Lincoln said. "Be sure you put your feet in the right place, then stand firm." The man went through a lot, but he was a better leader for it.

We are blessed. We are blessed to live in a free country where we have the right to our own thoughts, writing, speech, prayer, religion, and expression. We can vote, own property, and promote commerce. These rights may appear to be given to us on a red, white, and blue platter at birth, but they were earned. They were earned by the sacrifices of our United States military servicemen, servicewomen, and their families.

They were upheld by activists, philanthropists, politicians, lawyers, suffragettes, and everyday citizens who demanded more for our country and our children's future. Their sacrifices are honored each day in the lives of those civil servants and their partners who uphold the Constitution and the causes fought for and won by the American people. What a great honor it is to stand on the shoulders of giants and create the future of our country. Congratulations! You are now in a position to actively participate in creating that future. It's up to you to seize that opportunity!

The ones who are crazy enough to think that they
can change the world are the ones who do.
　　　　　—Steve Jobs

Brown, T., 2013, April 10, "The 2014 Budget Request: Agency by Agency," Retrieved from Federal Times: http://www.Federaltimes.com/article/20130410/AGENCY01/304100010/The-2014-budget-request-agency-by-agency.

Moore, J., 2014, January 16, 2014, "Funding: Agency-by-agency Breakdown of Spending Bill," Retrieved from Federal News Radio 1500am: http://www.Federalnewsradio.com/146/3543597/2014-funding-Agency-by-agency-breakdown-of-spending-bill.

"Mission Critical Opportunities for America—3rd Edition; WhereTheJobsAre.org," Partnership for Public Service.

"Education Levels for Fulltime/Non-seasonal Permanent Employees Hired in Fiscal Year 2013," Partnership for Public Service.

"Fulltime/Non-seasonal Employees Hired in Fiscal Year 2013," US Office of Personnel Management.

"Race and Ethnicity—Analysis for Fulltime/Non-seasonal, Permanent Employees Hired in Fiscal Year 2013," US Office of Personnel Management.

"Veterans in the Federal Executive Branch; Fiscal Year 2012," US Office of Personnel Management.

"Historical Federal Workforce Tables," US Office of Personnel Management.

"Historical Federal Workforce Tables," US Department of Commerce, Census Bureau.

"Civilian Labor Force: Population by Age, Sex and Race," US Department of Labor.

"Mission Critical Opportunities for America—3rd Edition," Partnership for Public Service, WhereTheJobsAre.org

O'Reilly, Megan, September 24, 2013, "LED Lighting Improves Sustainability for Specialty-Crop Producer," National Institute of Food And Agriculture, blogs.usda.gov.

"President Announces New Retirement Program from Treasury," February 3, 2014, US Department of Treasury.

APPENDIX— ADDITIONAL RÉSUMÉS

ADMINISTRATIVE ASSISTANT

Name

Address

Phone

E-mail

Work Experience

MM/YYYY–Present, PROFESSIONAL PROFILE, Career Summary, Hours/week: 40, Home Address

ADMINISTRATIVE SPECIALIST with more than 20 years of administrative management expertise in various business settings. Demonstrated expertise in project management, data analysis, information management, and improving operations. Proven analytical skills with the ability to investigate and evaluate facts and draw appropriate conclusions. Gifted communicator with dynamic interpersonal, oral, and written communication skills. Outstanding ability to establish priorities, multitask, and meet strict deadlines. Team player with strong organizational, research, and management skills and abilities. Proven proficiency in developing innovative solutions to problems and achieving results. Regarded in ability to handle confidential correspondence with the highest level of confidentially, prioritize tasks, meet time-sensitive deadlines, and work independently or with a team to achieve goals.

CLEARANCE: Understand the SF-86 and security clearance process; prepared to complete.

AREAS OF EXPERTISE: Workflow analysis; full range of office administrative principles, practices, methods, and techniques; accounting and finance; correspondence tracking: suspense and controlled correspondence; task management; information management; property accountability; document and report preparation; human resources; employee supervision; payroll; time and attendance; record and file maintenance; procurement of supplies and equipment; calendar management; coordination of travel; greet visitors and public officials; referrals; and excellent oral and written communication skills.

TECHNICAL SKILLS: Microsoft Office Suite (Word, Excel, Outlook, PowerPoint); Lotus; and expert ability to conduct credible Internet-based research.

ENDORSEMENTS:

TO BE LISTED HERE: A FEW SENTENCES ABOUT HOW GREAT YOU ARE FROM LINKEDIN, PERFORMANCE EVALUATIONS, AND LETTERS OF RECOMMENDATION.

MM/YYYY–Present, POSITION TITLE, Company, Hours/week: 40, Salary: $XX, Supervisor: Name, Phone

EXPERT ADMINISTRATIVE ASSISTANT, PLANNING AND EXECUTING WIDE RANGE OF ADMINISTRATIVE ACTIVITIES to ensure the optimal effectiveness of program operations. This includes, but is not limited to, receiving and screening telephone calls, facsimile transmissions, and visitors to the office and serving as point of contact. Coordinate meetings and assemble printed materials for meetings and briefings. Refer outside contacts to the appropriate persons, maintain hectic schedules and calendars, conduct timekeeping responsibilities, draft and proof letters, memos, and e-mail correspondence.

+++ Demonstrate high degree of professionalism, advanced organizational abilities, communication, and diplomacy skills.

MEETING COORDINATION: Assist the executive director in preparing for meetings, making appointments, and researching selected topics related to organization mission to educate, empower, and inspire youth with type 1 diabetes. Organize full logistics meetings. This includes, but is not limited to, arranging meeting room and equipment as needed and preparing paperwork. Perform follow-up activities.

ASSIST IN EVENT PLANNING AND COORDINATION: Support major fundraising events including a Benefit Luncheon in November 2014. Ensure proper transportation, accommodation, security, and credentials are set in advance for events and develop creative solutions during the planning as needed.

+++ Produced a slideshow presentation on PowerPoint with camper photos, sponsor logos, and honoree information as part of the main event for 350 attendees. As a result, $161,595 in donations was raised from the luncheon, compared to the $89,709 raised in 2013.

MAINTAIN AND ANALYZE OPERATIONS to ensure performance measures and objectives are achieved for desired levels of work quality and efficiency. Analyze and evaluate operations to develop and improve administrative policies, practices, and procedures. Make recommendations to senior-level management to support efforts to increase efficiency and effectiveness. Implement changes within delegated authority and ensure management-approved changes are implemented as instructed.

DATABASE MANAGEMENT: DESIGN TRACKING PROCEDURES for recordkeeping. Maintain employee records, including payroll and taxes. Develop and maintain records systems, including ticklers and logs. Assist with downloading data, assembling correspondence files, and reports for filing and maintaining.

+++ Successfully analyzed 6,000 records so different types of donations were easier to identify, and the data was easier to utilize in future fundraising and programming efforts.

WRITER/EDITOR: Maintain communications by writing, editing, and distributing press releases to media outlets in the Greater Atlanta area. Develop and communicate highly technical information using plain language and proper grammar for management reports. Compose and transcribe letters, interoffice memoranda, and interoffice reports, including confidential material. Participate in e-mail marketing webinars and in-person seminars on best practices when designing electronic newsletter.

+++ Develop a monthly newsletter in Constant Contact, which is distributed electronically to Camp Kudzu's constituents with updates on camp programming, information on fundraising and development opportunities, and medical information regarding type 1 diabetes.

DEVELOP AND MAINTAIN EFFECTIVE WORKING RELATIONSHIPS and partnerships. Communicate with team personnel to facilitate organizational goals. Work with the development team in facilitating the writing and distribution of fundraising letters to solicit donor support and thank contributors. Generate letter templates pertaining to a variety of constituents, compile mailing lists, and develop mail merges in Excel by using databases such as Raiser's Edge and Camp Brain.

MM/YYYY–MM/YYYY, POSITION TITLE, Company, Hours/week: 40, Salary: $XX, Supervisor: Name, Phone

FINANCE AND INVENTORY MANAGEMENT: Managed store money on a daily basis. Processed and replenished inventory on a weekly basis. Maintained an awareness and understanding of all product knowledge information, product promotions, upcoming sales and events, and advertised products.

PROVIDED EXEMPLARY CUSTOMER SERVICE through analysis of customer feedback and focusing of team's attention on areas requiring improvement.

IDENTIFIED CUSTOMER/CLIENT needs and partnered to fulfill those needs with products and services within sphere of influence. Worked independently to resolve problems. Used judgment regarding when to involve supervisors with resolving data issues.

EFFECTIVE ORAL COMMUNICATOR/TRAINER: Persuasively communicated ideas in person and by telephone with customer and company personnel. Appropriately tailored content to audience levels ranging from individual contributor to senior management.

MM/YYYY–MM/YYYY, POSITION TITLE, Company, Hours/week: 40, Salary: $XX, Supervisor: Name, Phone

DATA GATHERING, ANALYSIS, AND RECORD MANAGEMENT: CONDUCTED EXTENSIVE RESEARCH and drafted reports. Maintained the "Company of the Week" feature that provided examples of what FSR member financial institutions do to serve their communities, such as food drives and mentoring programs, on a weekly basis. Maintained records for 96 financial institutions, updating 15–25 records each week.

+++ Compiled and edited a 125-page 2013 Impact Report, highlighting the positive impact FSR member companies made in their local communities and nationwide through their community service and financial literacy efforts.

MEETING AND EVENT COORDINATION: Assisted in the coordination of and preparation for meetings and special events as part of Financial Literacy Month in April, including a panel discussion about the nonprofit Junior Achievement's 2014 survey on Teens and Personal Finance. Made 63 calls to Congress offices of the Financial and Economic Literacy Caucus on behalf of Financial Literacy day.

USED COMPUTER APPLICATIONS such as database management, word processing, and presentation software to produce a wide variety of materials to include. Updated and maintained contacts and FSR member company databases. Utilized the database, Salesforce, and Excel spreadsheets to organize the contact information of member companies who participated in community service projects and promoted financial literacy.

MM/YYYY–MM/YYYY, STUDENT, University, Hours/week: 40, Academic Advisor: Name, Phone

PROJECT COORDINATION SKILLS: Reviewed project requirements to effectively delegate tasks and establish time lines. Demonstrated skill in defining project scopes and details. Created project plans on conflict resolution by identifying tasks to be performed, necessary requirements, deliverables, and milestones. Recommended and devised individual scopes of work. Managed data and information collection and research. Monitored results in alignment with project goals and objectives. Actively encouraged communication, coordination, innovation, and high-quality team products.

INDEPENDENTLY RESEARCHED AND ANALYZED highly complex policy, strategy, and conceptual issues involving special topics in government and politics. Compiled and analyzed data to develop comprehensive research reports. Utilized resources for writing research papers, essays, and group presentations.

DEMONSTRATED EFFECTIVE COMMUNICATION: Prepared a wide variety of communications, both orally and in writing, to a wide variety of audiences on complex international affairs subject matters, conveying information in plain language using graphical aids to ensure common understanding. Prepared recommendations and presentations to support policy and project decisions.

DEVELOPED AND MAINTAINED EFFECTIVE RELATIONSHIPS: Assisted in conducting meetings with relevant team members, professors, and other industry professionals. Led teams for various projects using expert leadership and communication skills.

KEY PROJECTS:

+++ 12/2011–05/2013, As Student Activities Assistant: Implemented, executed, and evaluated on-campus events and off-campus trips. Events included movie screenings, club fairs, roller-skating nights, comedy nights, and trips to Philadelphia and New York City. Utilized problem-solving skills to remedy technical and logistical issues. Communicated with student body about events in the Philadelphia area by posting event information on Student Activities blog, Facebook page, and Twitter account. Presently the Facebook page has 758 members, and the Twitter page has 161 followers; this started from zero this started from zero in 2012.

+++ 01/2012–05/2013, As Leadership Empowerment and Advancement Program (LEAP) Student Coordinator: Applied leadership skills including meeting management, budgeting, conflict management, and team building. Maintained an alumni network blog with interviews from program graduates. Facilitated weekly workshops for a selective yearlong student leadership program, held office hours to review materials, sent weekly e-mails, and mentored students on leadership projects. As a result of my efforts, 14 LEAP Alumni were interviewed and five alumni guest speakers.

+++ Researched and authored a 42-page senior thesis, titled "Cooperation of Confrontation? After-School Programs' Strategies When Seeking Funding in Low-Income, Urban Areas." The paper received a grade of a 3.7 on a 4.0 scale (A).

MM/YYYY–MM/YYYY, SALES ASSOCIATE, Lord and Taylor, Kensington, MD (seasonal), Hours/week: 40, Salary: $XX, Supervisor: Name, Phone

ENSURED HIGH-LEVEL CUSTOMER SERVICE by providing a friendly environment that included greeting and acknowledging each customer and maintaining thorough product knowledge. Met targeted sales quotas. Maintained and balanced cash drawer. Assisted in organizing merchandise on the sales floor to appeal to customers. Performed clerical work in a variety of technical ways. Developed and fostered long-term, trusting relationships and shared information. Valued by management and colleagues for exceptional customer service practices.

+++ Ranked as part of the top 20 employees out of 150 full-time and part-time employees. The ranking was based on the amount of Lord & Taylor store credit cards opened per week and top sales per hour, which were calculated on a daily basis.

MM/YYYY–MM/YYYY, POSITION TITLE, Company, Hours/week: 40, Salary: $XX, Supervisor: Name, Phone

EDUCATION POLICY: Worked with a six-person intern team to establish environmental science lesson plans for two seven-week camps by the Washington DC Housing Authority. Lesson plans were separated by age level: five- and six-year-olds, and seven-to-ten-year-olds. Weekly themes included Pollination, the Water Cycle, and NASA.

+++ Contributed by writing lesson plans for campers at a DC House Authority home twice a week. The camp occurred in July and August, and the activities I brainstormed and scheduled occurred over the course of the summer. Activities included arts and crafts, playing circle games, and reading stories dealing with the themes.

MEASURED CAMPER PERFORMANCE THROUGH VARIOUS EVALUATING METHODS, ensuring performance requirements, program policies, learning objectives, and goals were accurately followed. Used problem-resolution skills to adapt to ever-changing educational environment.

CONDUCTED RESEARCH on establishing a Montessori-style nursery school for two-to-five-year-olds in fall 2012. Visited Montessori schools in the Washington, DC area and interviewed teacher guides and principals. Compiled a report outlining the guidelines establishing a Montessori school, as well as a curriculum for the students.

MM/YYYY–MM/YYYY, POSITION TITLE, Company, Hours/week: 40, Salary: $XX, Supervisor: Name, Phone

STRATEGIC COMMUNICATIONS: Interned as part of advanced Haverford research seminar on grassroots politics in Philadelphia. Wrote a final research paper about the mobilization campaign supporting Special Education Funding in Pennsylvania. Updated social media websites weekly including the Pennsylvania School Talk (PA School Talk), Facebook, and Twitter.

EDUCATION

Bachelor of Arts, Political Science Minor: Creative Writing, University, City, State

Thesis: "Cooperation or Confrontation? After-School Programs' Strategies When Seeking Funding in Low-Income, Urban Areas" (September 2012–May 2013)

ATTORNEY

Name

Address

Phone

E-mail

MM/YYYY–Present, PROFESSIONAL PROFILE, Career Summary, Hours/week: 40, Home Address

SENIOR EXECUTIVE/GOVERNMENT AFFAIRS/ATTORNEY with more than 15 years of experience providing vast executive team, profit and loss, and strategic development expertise in the health care industry, and wide-ranging experience in public policy, government affairs, regulation, and board governance. Experienced in leading change and people through high-profile transitions using expertise in business and political acumen. Demonstrated experience developing cost-effective strategies to reach key constituencies, particularly in the area of innovative small businesses. Recognized for outstanding communication and negotiation skills at all levels of the organization, flexibility, keen political savvy, leadership abilities, and sense of humor.

CLEARANCE: Understand the SF-86 and security clearance process; prepared to complete.

AREAS OF EXPERIENCE: Driving results; coalition building; political savvy; intergovernmental affairs; health care delivery; health care systems; strategic communications; crisis communication; public affairs; government relations; strategic planning; federal budgeting; administrative management; training; mentoring; coaching; stem education; leveraging diversity; low-income health insurance programs; program evaluation and management; project lifecycle management; document review; ethics; process improvement and simplification; team and project leadership; quantitative/qualitative analysis; risk and feasibility assessment; technical, legal, regulatory, and best-practices research; policy analysis; stakeholder/customer/client relations; and oral and written communication skills.

TECHNICAL SKILLS: Microsoft Office Suite (Word, Excel, PowerPoint, Outlook); ability to conduct credible research using the Internet.

ENDORSEMENTS:

TO BE LISTED HERE: A FEW SENTENCES ABOUT HOW GREAT YOU ARE FROM LINKEDIN, PERFORMANCE EVALUATIONS, AND LETTERS OF RECOMMENDATION.

MM/YYYY–MM/YYYY, POSITION TITLE, Company, Hours/week: 40, Salary: $XX, Supervisor: Name, Phone

EXPERT PROJECT AND PROGRAM MANAGER: Provide project management leadership and direction for a portfolio of significant high-visibility and broad-scope projects. Oversee all operations and strategic initiatives, legal affairs, compliance, profit and loss, new business development, and project management on federal and state government contracts within specific areas of expertise, including quality measures reporting. Recommend organizational change management strategies by developing reports, conducting analytical studies, and developing strategic development plans. Extensive experience working with innovative small businesses, including high-growth, start-up companies.

+++ Expert on organizational and program management theories, principles and techniques, and expert ability to manage a diverse and complex organization.

STRATEGIC COMMUNICATIONS AND PLANNING: Develop and implement strategic communication plans with an emphasis on public advocacy stakeholder communication, messaging, outreach, and public relations. Expert at planning, developing, managing, and assessing programmatic functions within legal, legislative, and other large government and nonprofit service entities.

CONTRACT MANAGER AND NEGOTIATOR: Simultaneously provide oversight for multiple contracts, adjusting and reprioritizing workload as needed. Develop and review language for Statements of Work (SOW), proposals, quotes, and contracts. Consistently ensure performance according to contract specifications (scope of work), quality standards, budget, and schedule, and submit timely reports of technical progress against performance metrics. Apply knowledge of grants and contracts, fiscal management, and budget preparation while negotiating legally and politically sensitive issues.

BUDGET AND FINANCE MANAGEMENT: Manage a $5 million budget. Adhere to budget guidelines for program expenses and fulfill contract terms. Monitor expenditures and use cost-benefit thinking to set priorities. Analyze need for various operations and make recommendations to senior management on resource allocation. Keen understanding of financial processes.

ANALYZE STATUTORY AND REGULATORY FRAMEWORK of various federal and state laws to determine consistency of programs with the existing legal structure. Based on this analysis, propose policies to facilitate the operation of the programs within the legal framework and remove barriers to entry of capital into the program. Conduct legal research on complex factual, legal, and policy issues. Research a wide variety of issues and interpret legislative and other regulatory guidance to create various documents.

PROVIDE TECHNICAL AND ADMINISTRATIVE SUPERVISION to subordinate staff. Ensure that company policies and priorities are being followed. Develop performance standards and evaluate work performance of subordinates. Skill in leading, supervising, evaluating, and developing a diverse staff of professionals and keen ability to coordinate complex tasks and teams, including partnerships with other entities. Oversee assignment of work and managing of workflow and resources.

EXCELLENT ORAL AND WRITTEN COMMUNICATION AND PUBLIC SPEAKING SKILLS with an ability to convey information concerning complex programs and functions, and effectively address sensitive topics with various audiences. Communicate effectively with managers and executives to identify projects and outcomes to ensure alignment of strategic goals and objectives with company mission. Write clear, concise material for various audiences. Provide translation of complex, highly technical concepts into simple, plain language.

MM/YYYY–MM/YYYY, POSITION TITLE, Company, Hours/week: 40, Salary: $XX, Supervisor: Name, Phone

PROVIDED PROGRAM LEADERSHIP AND DIRECTION: LED CHANGE, STRATEGIC PLANNING, AND ORGANIZATIONAL REDESIGN for Commission on Accreditation of Health Care Management Education (CAHME), an organization focusing on accreditation of graduate health care management programs in institutions of higher education. Introduced a strategic vision to globalize CAHME accreditation. Served ex officio on CAHME Board of Directors and effectively managed programs and other innovative initiatives, providing guidance, direction, and development of ideas to various stakeholders to accomplish the mission of ensuring program services were effectively promoted, implemented, and evaluated.

+++ Demonstrated knowledge of universities and other academic institutions of higher education where science, technology, engineering, and mathematics (STEM) research and education research are conducted.

EXPLOITED THE USE OF TECHNOLOGY TO IMPROVE OPERATIONAL EFFECTIVENESS AND EFFICIENCY. Used knowledge of change management techniques to streamline several high-cost programs to operate more efficiently. Aligned and integrated such strategies with external organizations and resources for effective mission execution. Improved functionality and use of CAHME's new electronic Accreditation System; trained program directors and CAHME site visitors on effective use of the system.

+++ Implemented change-management plan for organization to begin using electronic format communication. Within three months, successfully turned the organization around so that all communication was electronic and an easily accessible database was established and maintained. Stakeholders responded positively to this change, helping immeasurably in changing the attitudes of the staff and board of directors.

PRINCIPAL ADVISOR TO AN EXECUTIVE ON ADMINISTRATIVE MATTERS AFFECTING THE ORGANIZATION. Advised Board on organizational programs and operations, including, but not limited to: strategic and organization planning, budget formulation and execution, resource management, project management, and the measurement of outcomes. Worked directly and effectively with executive level management in the identification and formulation of strategies and approaches. Used technical expertise in strategic planning to make recommendations to management on key initiatives, policies, procedures, guidelines, and processes requiring improvement.

BUDGET MANAGEMENT AND ANALYSIS: Created and managed a $1 million budget. Assumed ultimate profit and loss responsibility in operational and capital budgets, implementing changes to lower CAHME operating costs while increasing revenue. Used excellent BUSINESS MANAGEMENT SKILLS in the areas of finance, resource allocation, and leveraging of resources to manage financial processes. Provided detailed monthly expense reports.

+++ Used expert BUSINESS ACUMEN to develop internal controls integrated into day-to-day operations to minimize the potential for fraud, waste, and abuse. Extensive knowledge of principles, theories, and practices of financial analysis with an emphasis on development of operating guides and cost-accounting procedures.

LED CROSS-FUNCTIONAL TEAMS: Collaboratively managed large teams of volunteer academicians and practitioners as well as paid staff to promote the application of competency-based criteria for accreditation in graduate-level health care management education. Provided team and individual leadership toward meeting vision, mission, and goals in an inclusive workplace that facilitated cooperation and teamwork. Fostered the development of others and supported constructive resolution of conflicts.

MM/YYYY–MM/YYYY, POSITION TITLE, Company, Hours/week: 40, Salary: $XX, Supervisor: Name, Phone

HEALTH CARE EXTERNAL AFFAIRS AND LEGAL EXECUTIVE: Inspected and reviewed projects to monitor compliance with goals and objectives. Spearheaded development and ongoing execution of Capitol Hill, DHHS, and 50-state advocacy plans to incorporate URAC accreditation into mandated health insurance exchanges.

EXPERT LEGAL ADVISOR ON FEDERAL REGULATIONS AND POLICY: Consistently provided strategic advice on politically sensitive board governance matters and engaged in complex legal contractual negotiations. Provided impartial advice and rendered legal opinions, both written and oral, based on extensive research and analyses of federal, state, and local regulations and policies. Appropriately handled sensitive, highly confidential matters with discretion and maintained confidential records in accordance with regulations and confidentiality policies.

+++ Significantly enhanced URAC's alliance development efforts, resulting in cohosting revenue-generating policy symposia and white paper development in the areas of medication adherence, mental health parity, and Wall Street investor forums.

EXPERT BUSINESS ACUMEN: STRATEGICALLY MANAGED HUMAN, FINANCIAL, AND INFORMATION RESOURCES. Consistently utilized a consensus-based management style, while also bearing responsibility for capital budgets and profit and loss in multimillion-dollar operations. Oversaw and delivered fair and balanced performance appraisals to subordinate staff.

DEMONSTRATED RESULTS-DRIVEN LEADERSHIP: Performed complex analyses to determine problematic root issues and develop sound, legal solutions to overcome them. Demonstrated ability to meet organizational goals and customer expectations. Made decisions that produced high-quality results by applying technical knowledge, analyzing problems, and calculating risks.

LED TEAMS AND BUILT PARTNERSHIPS: Collaboratively managed large teams of clinicians and professional staff to achieve and exceed annual corporate scorecard goals. Established, influenced, and maintained effective relationships with internal and external stakeholders, including senior-level executives and other professionals. Established collaborative team mission, vision, and strategic objectives and priorities. Oversaw team function, facility requirements, and global location assessment. Used expertise in coaching, mentoring, ensuring, diversity, conflict management, and team building. Expert ability to form coalitions through education on conflictual aspects of any given issue.

+++ Set in motion a collaborative coalition among national stakeholders, including major pharmaceutical and drug store corporations, as well as academe, to lead the creation of a conference on medication adherence, which attracted national media coverage.

EXPERT COMMUNICATOR AND PUBLIC SPEAKER: Prepared and delivered speeches before government and public groups, and directly responded to congressional and other inquiries. Conducted Senate and House briefings designed to educate Congress on the importance of the growing field of medication-adherence programs. Scheduled these briefings after the policy conference and coauthored a scholarly white paper on the subject, to make conference findings and best practices in the field available to all.

MM/YYYY–MM/YYYY, POSITION TITLE, Company, Hours/week: 40, Salary: $XX, Supervisor: Name, Phone

LED PEOPLE: DIRECTED, OVERSAW, AND COORDINATED THE WORK OF SUBORDINATES. Oversaw strategic planning and management, budget preparation, staff recruitment and supervision, and managed competitive review of proposals for awards. Formulated policies and strategies that guided training and development programs. Conducted analysis and studies to determine the effectiveness and development of instructional and training programs.

DEVELOPED AND MANAGED CHAMBER POLICY ON HEALTH AND LIFE SCIENCES and advocated those policies before Congress and federal agencies. Created and lobbied life sciences policy platform on adult and pediatric vaccines; follow-on biologics; Medicare part D noninterference; direct-to-consumer advertising; drug safety; Prescription Drug User Fee Act; Medical Device User Fee Modernization Act; clinical trials; importation; critical path; patent reform; and disease management. Managed and lobbied Chamber's general health policy platform, including comparative effectiveness research; health information technology; Medicare reimbursement; provider pay-for-performance; health care quality measures; consumer-directed health care; State Children's Health Insurance Program (CHIP); and health courts. Evaluated legislative and regulatory information related to CHIP to assess impact on the organization policies.

COMMUNICATED EFFECTIVELY AND BUILT COALITIONS INTERNALLY AND EXTERNALLY and with other federal agencies, state and local governments, nonprofit and private-sector organizations, foreign governments, and international organizations to achieve common goals. Represented US Chamber of Commerce to relevant external groups and fostered partnerships with other divisions, directorates, federal agencies, scientific organizations, and the academic community at large. Actively collaborated with major pharmaceutical and insurance corporations, as well as large trade associations in the medical device and health insurance industries. Drafted comments and key-vote letters, and testified concerning federal legislation and regulation.

MM/YYYY–MM/YYYY, POSITION TITLE, Company, Hours/week: 40, Salary: $XX, Supervisor: Name, Phone

MANAGED STRATEGIC PLANNING AND DELIVERY OF PUBLIC POLICY INITIATIVES, including those concerning legislative, regulatory, and international matters. Ensured Medicare and Medicaid reimbursement advocacy coincided with corporate strategic objectives and priorities. Lobbied Senate to ensure Congress's passage of flu-vaccine liability protections. Drafted policy statements, guidelines, issue papers, and procedural instructions and protocols to improve and implement new initiatives.

MM/YYYY–MM/YYYY, POSITION TITLE, Company, Hours/week: 40, Salary: $XX, Supervisor: Name, Phone

MANAGED STATE POLICY OPERATIONS for several domestic regions, focusing on policy and governmental affairs matters. Provided counsel to state government affairs division for regulatory, legislative, and antitrust matters. Managed and contributed to governmental-affairs task forces, initiatives, and policy work groups, with particular emphasis on Medicaid, Medicare Modernization Act, State Children's Health Insurance Program, reimbursement, importation, price controls, tort reform, direct-to-consumer advertising, trade secrets, and multistate purchasing agreements. Frequently testified before state legislatures and regulatory agencies in support of industry priorities. Conducted legal research and drafted memoranda and comments on state and federal regulations. Provided technical advice related to health care coverage for low-income children and adults to stakeholders (i.e., beneficiary groups, providers, and advocacy groups).

EDUCATION

Juris Doctor, University City, State, Zip

Bachelor of Arts, Political Science, University, City, State

LICENSURE

Washington, DC and Maryland Bars

FINANCIAL AND BUDGET ANALYST

Name

Address

Phone

E-mail

Work Experience

MM/YYYY–Present, PROFESSIONAL PROFILE, Career Summary, Home Address, Hours/week: 40

FINANCIAL/BUDGET ANALYST with more than 15 years of progressive experience providing analysis, strategic planning, program, and project management. Expertise in strategic and tactical planning, program and management analysis, and resource analysis and optimization. Solid record of performance managing analytical studies, key initiatives, and high-profile performance improvement projects. Technical expert and analyst on complex program issues. Very strong critical-thinking, problem-solving, research, and liaison skills. Recognized for outstanding communication skills, flexibility, keen political savvy, sense of humor, and leadership abilities.

CLEARANCE: Defense Industrial Security Office (DISCO)—Top Secret/SCI (TS/SCI)

AREAS OF EXPERTISE: Program evaluation and management; project lifecycle management; budget analysis; financial planning and management; administrative management; strategic and operations planning; cash flow analysis; workforce analysis and planning; operational, compliance auditing; internal control reviews; cost analysis; process improvement and simplification; team and project leadership; quantitative/qualitative analysis; training; risk and feasibility assessment; technical, regulatory, and best-practices research; policy analysis; and excellent oral and written communication skills.

TECHNICAL SKILLS: Microsoft Office Suite (Word, Excel, Access, Outlook, PowerPoint); and expert ability to conduct credible Internet-based research.

ENDORSEMENTS

TO BE LISTED HERE: A FEW SENTENCES ABOUT HOW GREAT YOU ARE FROM LINKEDIN, PERFORMANCE EVALUATIONS, AND LETTERS OF RECOMMENDATION.

MM/YYYY–MM/YYYY, POSITION TITLE, Company, Hours/week: 40, Salary: $XX, Supervisor: Name, Phone

CERTIFIED PROJECT MANAGER PROFESSIONAL with excellent business acumen in the areas of finance, resource allocation, and leveraging of technical resources. Oversaw daily operations of charge number management, invoice verification, and SPA initiations. Provided exceptional client service by assessing client needs, maintaining high-quality standards, and evaluating client satisfaction. Developed, implemented, and oversaw control policies and procedures. Prepared basis of project estimate for pricing and cost proposals. Dealt with challenging client issues, resolving them by implementing win-win solutions.

+++ Facilitated due diligence and post-close activities for multimillion-dollar acquisitions. Moved to an offsite location to work directly with the acquired company. Audited billing and revenue documents for active contracts. Set up a Project Control department and created Estimate at Completions (EACs) for IDIQ contracts and standalone contracts. As a result, the acquisition was approved, and the management was able to accurately monitor revenue recognition.

EXPERT FINANCIAL AND BUDGET ANALYST: Performed a wide variety of analytical duties related to budget formulation, justification, presentation, execution, and review of financial programs. Conducted cost-benefit analysis of deliverables under established budgets and alternative budgets to provide recommendations to authorized and interested sources based upon results. Provided advice and assistance to managers in the development and presentation of budget requests. Prepared monthly and biweekly project reporting. Monitored obligations incurred and expenditures incurred for variance analysis. Reviewed a variety of historical data to prepare budget estimates for various projects.

+++ Assisted program and division managers with schedule creation by developing financial reports, performance and profitability analysis, and project estimates.

CONTRACT MANAGEMENT AND ADMINISTRATION: Oversaw completion of contract deliverables, EACs at each period close, and reviewed EACs and guided senior leadership based on report data. Analyzed and reviewed cost estimates for CPAF, CPFF, FFP, FPLOE, and T&M contracts. Consistently ensured performance according to contract specifications (scope of work), quality standards, budget, and schedule, and submitted timely reports of technical progress against performance metrics.

+++ Supported largest volume of Firm Fixed Price contracts with $68 million estimated negotiated value.

DIRECT SUPERVISOR: Directed and mentored up to 16 project control analysts. Recruited, hired, and trained new team members as well as assessed and reassigned workloads to ensure optimal support to program managers. Keen ability to coordinate complex tasks and teams, including partnerships with other entities. Oversaw performance management for each employee: development and evaluation of performance plans, mentoring and coaching for Individual Development Plans, and performance counseling and coaching. Took disciplinary action when necessary to ensure acceptable conduct and completion of operations according to established procedures.

+++ Recognized as an expert in providing effective, low-cost solutions to complex issues. Promoted to lead, support, and train 43 project controllers across seven operations within a business unit.

PRICE AND COST ANALYSIS: Conducted qualitative and quantitative analysis of complex data and conveyed information in a variety of written formats including cost-benefit analysis and future-value analysis. Synthesized data into coherent and comprehensive reports demonstrating effectiveness and efficiency of current contracts and viability of implementing new ones as part of persuasive acquisition strategies. Performed pre- and postaward contracting functions including price/cost analysis, negotiations, administration, and termination for supplies, services, materials, and equipment.

ENSURED PERFORMANCE METRICS AND MEASURES were achieved, often exceeding desired levels. Provided expert oversight for the successful completion of projects, and analyzed metrics to track performance. Monitored results versus targets and provided gap-analysis to achieve strategic goals and performance objectives. Consistently met or exceeded management and organizational strategic goals and objectives through implementation of short- and long-term projects and action plans.

RESEARCH AND ANALYSIS: Independently researched and prepared analyses on a broad range of subjects. Researched and analyzed financial data for external and internal clients. Provided budgetary information to assist project managers in implementing organizational policies. Prepared weekly and monthly budgetary reports for upper management. Collected, retrieved, and analyzed date to resolve financial discrepancies. Created and maintained budgetary reports using spreadsheets and database programs. Analyzed program requirements to ensure compliance with budgetary allocations.

+++ Distributed current financial reporting data and utilized automatic EAC templates to improve financial reporting accuracy. Provided assistance and training on using EAC templates.

+++ Forecasted financial data for programs, created EACs, and created and maintained PAN funding spreadsheets.

INTERPRETED REGULATIONS: Ensured that projects were properly documented and adhered to guidelines. Applied guidelines, procedures, policies, and regulations related to program and project funding and budget, such as tracking program and project costs, allocations, apportionments, and funding and cost limitations. Extensive knowledge of Federal Acquisition Regulation (FAR) and all phases of the federal budget process to develop budget estimates in prescribed program budgeting systems and conventional line-item format, including a thorough understanding of policies, directives, and regulations.

BUILT AND MAINTAINED EFFECTIVE WORKING RELATIONSHIPS in a team environment. Professionally represented the company of a team, developing goals and performance measures to encourage and assess the success of projects. Educated, advised, negotiated, and collaborated with stakeholders to build support for ideas and initiatives, tactfully and diplomatically addressing issues that were in contention or sensitive. Communicated with senior management and procurement, budgeting, and financial operations teams.

+++ Worked with project controllers to accurately diagnose and resolve all issues and streamline project control processes. Identified issues and drove corrective actions and investigated new technologies to improve efficiency.

+++ Coordinated support, SG-20, and SOX requirements with project control analysts, contracts, subcontracts, accounts receivable, finance, and accounts payable groups.

EXPERT ORAL AND WRITTEN COMMUNICATION SKILLS: Prepared communication materials and analytical reports for publication and distribution in support of projects. Conducted meetings and provided presentations to groups and individuals using appropriate software and superior communication skills. Wrote, edited, and presented status reports, working papers, briefings, strategic plans, and proposals. Generated clear and succinct daily, weekly, monthly, and quarterly financial and forecasting reports. Prepared draft proposals for procedural changes and modifications to improve the effectiveness of processes.

EDUCATION

Master of Science, University, City, State, Zip

Bachelor of Science, University, City, State, Zip

JOB-RELATED TRAINING

RLN Development, Earned Value Management

Deltek Cobra, Deltek Costpoint, Hyperion, MS Office, MS Project, SAP

INFORMATION TECHNOLOGY PROJECT MANAGER

Name

Address

E-mail

Phone

Work Experience

MM/YYYY–Present, PROFESSIONAL PROFILE, Career Summary, Home Address, Hours/week: 40

INFORMATION TECHNOLOGY (IT) PROJECT MANAGER with more than 20 years of progressive experience providing IT services, program and project management, and analysis and strategic planning. Solid record of performance managing high-value, high-profile projects. A persistent leader with strong business acumen and proven ability to balance short-term priorities against long-term organizational goals. Very strong critical-thinking, problem-solving, research, and liaison skills. Recognized for outstanding communication skills, flexibility, keen political savvy, leadership abilities, and a sense of humor.

CLEARANCE: Understand the SF-86 and security clearance process; prepared to complete.

AREAS OF EXPERTISE: Information technology management; telecommunications; embedded operating systems; data management; program evaluation and management; wireless network infrastructure systems; network security; information security; information management; systems analysis; systems administration; strategic and operations planning; workforce analysis and planning; process improvement and simplification; team and project leadership; quantitative/qualitative analysis; risk and feasibility assessment; regulatory and best-practices research; policy analysis; and excellent oral and written communication skills.

TECHNICAL EXPERTISE: 2G (iDEN), 3G (WCDMA), and LTE Wireless Network Technology, Satellite Communications Technology (GEO); Software and Hardware Development Processes (Embedded Systems); and expert ability to conduct credible Internet-based research.

INTERNATIONAL BUSINESS EXPERIENCE: In-depth knowledge of national and international regulatory policies affecting radio spectrum management in order to ensure compliance with national- and international-level rules and regulations.

EUROPE: UNITED KINGDOM, GERMANY—For INMARSAT meetings and customer interface meetings relating to terrestrial-based satellite communications.

CIS/RUSSIA: KIEV, UKRAINE AND MOSCOW, RUSSIA—Sales Agent/Customer meetings for Land Mobile Satellite Application Development.

ASIA: TAIWAN, JAPAN, SINGAPORE—Various project and engineering meetings for wireless- and satellite-based product design and development.

SOUTH AMERICA: COLOMBIA, MEXICO, BRAZIL, PERU, AND ARGENTINA—Technical Project Lead Activities: customer meetings for Land Mobile SATCOM Applications, wireless network interoperability testing, and assessment of field performance defects.

SOFTWARE: Microsoft Office Suite (Word, Excel, Outlook, PowerPoint, Visio, Project), Android OS

METHODOLOGIES: SDLC, Software Capability Maturity Modeling

PLATFORMS: Mobile Location Server (Motorola), Over-the-Air Mobile Device Data Management (Giesecke and Devrient—Mobile SIM Card manufacturer), Openwave Media Access Gateway (Mobile Browser Services), Mobile Messaging Servers (Open Mobile Alliance standard)

INTERNET: SIP (Session Initiated Protocol), TCP/IP, IPv4

DATABASES: Radius, Oracle

ENDORSEMENTS:

TO BE LISTED HERE: A FEW SENTENCES ABOUT HOW GREAT YOU ARE FROM LINKEDIN, PERFORMANCE EVALUATIONS, AND LETTERS OF RECOMMENDATION.

MM/YYYY–MM/YYYY, POSITION TITLE, Company, Hours/week: 40, Salary: $XX, Supervisor: Name, Phone

PMP-CERTIFIED PROJECT MANAGER for lab integration testing on an assignment focused on working with a team of engineers and management staff to coordinate the testing of software and hardware components for 4G/LTE services. Captured project time lines and milestone scheduling using tools such as MS Excel and MS Project for weekly team and management updates. Efficiently led projects by applying comprehensive knowledge of Systems Development Life Cycle (SDLC) methodology and project management principles, concepts, techniques, and methods for IT systems and software design, development, and modification. Provided expert advice on situations and issues that involved innovative solutions, methods, and practices to align with business requirements.

+++ Provided the client with weekly project milestone status and other updates using tools such as MS Project and MS Excel. The client's technical team successfully completed software validation and verification testing of a key LTE RAN network element for commercial release to the US market.

TELECOMMUNICATIONS EXPERTISE: Evaluate, analyze, develop, manage, and improve communications systems, procedures, and requirements. Demonstrate knowledge of current developments and trends in communications concepts and technology. Keen understanding of a wide range of wireless communications theories, concepts, principles, practices, procedures, policies, standards, and operational requirements. Evaluate devices, proposals, and approaches to ensure performance characteristics of wireless communications equipment, systems, services, and transmission media.

BUDGET OVERSIGHT: Performed purchase requisition services for the technical team to acquire critical test equipment and software tools necessary to perform validation and verification testing of new features and services. Developed excellent relations with key vendors to ensure timely deliveries. Tracked lab purchase expenditures against budget allocations for monthly management updates. Formulated, forecasted, and monitored budgets to correspond with the planning of several IT projects and operations, applying knowledge of contracting procedures and legal requirements, cost analyses, and budgets.

ESTABLISHED WORKING RELATIONS with staff of the prime RAN (Radio Access Network) equipment vendor (Alcatel-Lucent) to coordinate lab entry and lab exit testing criteria and milestone development scheduling with the Tier 1 team members. Worked closely with technical staff and senior management to identify and mitigate risks to project time lines.

MM/YYYY–MM/YYYY, POSITION TITLE, Company, Hours/week: 40, Salary: $XX, Supervisor: Name, Phone

IT ARCHITECT: Assisted in establishing a structure and technical process to deliver quality end-user devices to achieve a competitive market position. Software model for the end product was a client-server type with complex OTA (over-the-air) protocols for network operations (such as wide-band CDMA) and TCP/IP based for end-user, value-added services as implemented via packet data operations. Knowledge of the customary approaches, techniques, and requirements appropriate to an assigned computer applications area or computer specialty area in an organization; planning the sequence of actions necessary to accomplish the assignment where this entailed coordination with others outside the organizational unit and development of project controls; and adaptation of guidelines and precedents to the needs of the assignment.

VALIDATED AND VERIFIED PROCESSES AND PROCEDURES: Designed and developed processes and procedures necessary to implement subscriber device network validation and verification. Meticulously analyzed entire process through implementation, as well as, all documentation. Conducted thorough interviews of staff, documenting findings that focused on requirements outlined in the Statement of Work (SOW), and verified that all employees and processes abided by project management methodologies and leading practices. Accurately documented all findings and compiled into a detailed report. Analyzed information and evaluated results to choose the best solution and solve problems. Knowledge of operational and performance characteristics of wireless communications in developing procedures, policies, and practices for local use.

TEAM LEADER AND MEMBER: Established working relations with the Product Management groups in the NII markets (Brazil, Mexico, Peru, Chile, and Argentina) to understand and coordinate handset portfolio development and product realization. This team consisted of about 20 staff members across all markets.

SUPERIOR TIME MANAGEMENT skills afford the time to assist and collaborate with colleagues as well as across departments. Communicated with supervisors, peers, and subordinates, providing information to supervisors, coworkers, and subordinates by telephone, in written form, e-mail, or in person.

+++ Consistently established effective priorities among opposing requirements and setting criteria and standards.

DOCUMENTING/RECORDING INFORMATION: Entered and recorded information in written and electronic form. Analyzed data and information by identifying the underlying principles, reasons, and facts of information by breaking down information and data into separate parts. Processed information, compiled, coded, categorized, calculated, tabulated, audited, and verified information and data.

DEMONSTRATED ORAL AND WRITTEN COMMUNICATION: DEVELOPED AND FINALIZED REPORTS, manuals, standard operating procedures, and briefings, ensuring material was properly formatted and edited for grammar and plain language usage. Professionally represented company in all interactions.

MM/YYYY–MM/YYYY, POSITION TITLE, Company, Hours/week: 40, Salary: $XX, Supervisor: Name, Phone

TECHNICAL PROJECT LEAD for Nextel's iDEN Subscriber Device Development group. Oversaw coordination and communications with Nextel's handset vendors (Motorola and Boost Mobile) to realize new product portfolio offerings for Nextel customer base. Secured cooperation, competitiveness, and motivation from all parties involved, particularly between companies, which resulted in major growth of new subscribers and multimillion-dollar profits from new services. Ensured acceptable conduct and completion of operations according to established procedures. Applied basic RF engineering theory and operating principles to the application of existing and planned technology to communications requirements, equipment interoperability, and compatibility.

+++ Developed successful network acceptance and product launch of the following handsets/network services: MMS (Multimedia messaging), Openwave Web Browser, and enhancements to Nextel's flagship Push-to-Talk technology which allows Dynamic Group Calling (on the fly).

+++ Developed and implemented verification and testing plans to successfully achieve network acceptance for new products and services to allow commercial market launch of more than 10 new wireless handset models. Secured a cooperative team environment, which resulted in major growth of new subscribers and increased revenue at the multimillion-dollar level with the new road map offerings.

IT PROJECT MANAGEMENT: Provided hands-on management of entire project lifecycle from initial needs assessment through implementation and full-scale launch. Proposed and initiated new processes, projects, and programs to be implemented. Developed, reviewed, and analyzed technical program data and information, such as specification guides, concept papers, and justifications in support of acquisition operations.

LED CROSS-FUNCTIONAL TEAMS AND PEOPLE of more than 20 people. Led multiorganizational planning and communication tasks with internal groups such as product management, technology/architecture, verification testing, RF engineering, network engineering, customer care, technical sales, and marketing groups for the planning of new handset road maps and network service offerings. Keen ability to coordinate complex tasks and teams, including partnerships with other entities.

INFORMATION SECURITY (INFOSEC): Ensured confidentiality, integrity, and availability of systems, networks, and data through planning, analysis, development, implementation, maintenance, and enhancement of information systems security programs, policies, and procedures. Developed and practiced information security protocol required to protect systems.

PROVIDED EXEMPLARY CUSTOMER SERVICE through analysis of customer feedback and focusing of team attention on areas requiring improvement.

IDENTIFIED CUSTOMER/CLIENT needs and partnered to fulfill those needs with products and services within sphere of influence. Valued by management for exceptional customer service practices.

TROUBLESHOOTING AND PROBLEM SOLVING/RESOLUTION: Identified problems and determined accuracy and relevance of information. Used sound judgment to generate and evaluate alternatives and make recommendations. Interacted effectively in situations where frequent changes, delays, and unexpected events arose that caused major shifts in priorities, timetables, and work assignments. Reviewed, analyzed, and resolved difficult and complex technical problems involving systems compatibility, both installation-wide and external interoperability, of voice and packet-data circuits, distribution, satellite linkages, and networking. Demonstrated a wide range of communications concepts, principles, and practices to accomplish work processes through the use of telecommunications devices, methods, services, and facilities.

EDUCATION

Master of Science, Engineering Science, University, City, State, Zip

Bachelor of Science, Electrical Engineering, University, City, State, Zip

ADDITIONAL INFORMATION

CERTIFICATIONS

+ ISO:9001:2000 Internal Quality Systems Auditor, 9/2002—9/2002, BSI/CEEM, Lisle, IL

+ Project Management Professional, 9/2009—9/2009, Project Management Institute, Washington, DC

AWARDS

Name

Address

Phone

E-mail

Work Experience

MM/YYYY–Present, PROFESSIONAL PROFILE, Career Summary, Hours/week: 40

CLEARANCE: TOP SECRET W/SCI ELIGIBILITY

BUSINESS PROFESSIONAL with more than 10 years of progressive experience providing analysis, strategic planning, program, and project management. Expertise in strategic and tactical planning, program and management analysis, and resource analysis and optimization. Solid record of performance managing analytical studies, key initiatives, and high-profile performance-improvement projects. Technical expert and analyst on complex program issues. Very strong critical-thinking, problem-solving, research, and liaison skills. Recognized for outstanding communication skills, flexibility, keen political savvy, sense of humor, and leadership abilities.

AREAS OF EXPERTISE: Operations management; logistics; program evaluation and management; project lifecycle management; strategic and operations planning; database administration; workforce analysis and planning; process improvement and simplification; team and project leadership; quantitative/qualitative analysis; risk and feasibility assessment; technical, regulatory, and best-practices research; policy analysis; negotiating; and excellent oral and written communication skills.

TECHNICAL SKILLS: Microsoft Office Suite (Word, Excel, Outlook, PowerPoint); and expert ability to conduct credible Internet-based research.

ENDORSEMENTS:

TO BE LISTED HERE: A FEW SENTENCES ABOUT HOW GREAT YOU ARE FROM LINKEDIN, PERFORMANCE EVALUATIONS, AND LETTERS OF RECOMMENDATION.

MM/YYYY–MM/YYYY, POSITION TITLE, Company, Hours/week: 40, Salary: $XX, Supervisor: Name, Phone

LOGISTICS PLANNING AND OPERATIONS MANAGEMENT: Oversee collection, detailed analysis, and reporting of all logistics activities supporting army units and equipment worldwide, including strategic deployments/redeployments. Identify all activities involved in providing needed logistical support. Integrate actions required of each activity into a comprehensive logistics plan in support of overall program plans. Work with a variety of military logistical concepts, practices, and procedures.

+++ Serve in a variety of roles: Deputy to the Chief of Current Operations; Retrograde Branch Chief; Primary Action Officer; and Liaison Officer to the ARSTAF.

PROGRAM MANAGEMENT, ANALYSIS, AND IMPROVEMENT: Review short- and long-term logistics planning goals. Develop and follow established processes to determine the effectiveness of current operations, determine problem areas, and propose solutions. Collect and analyze logistical data in the evaluation of various alternatives and make recommendations in regard to a potential path forward.

+++ Provided expert guidance and assistance in the management of complex projects, studies, and action items, keeping the director informed of critical developments and providing expert advice on administrative aspects.

+++ Team lead for biweekly Redistribution, Redeployment, Reset, Return and Disposal Council of Colonels and General Officer Steering Committees in support of retrograde drawdown in Afghanistan.

+++ Led small team of strategic planners and procurement analysts with expertise in Operational Contract Support (OCS).

CONTRACTING AND KNOWLEDGE OF CONTRACT TYPES: Supported strategic Department of the Army (DA) OCS planning, resourcing, and employment of contracting officers worldwide to ensure the most effective use of contingency-contracting assets. Possess knowledge of acquisition initiatives such as performance-based contracting, award-term contracting, and evaluation of past performance.

+++ Assisted with the oversight of DA OCS and Contingency Contracting strategic planning by Heads of Contracting Activities, Principal Assistants Responsible for Contracting, and Army contracting offices worldwide.

+++ Coordinated with Army G-3 Training Division and Headquarters Combined Arms Support Command to correct deficiencies with the Operational Contract Support course at the Army Logistics University. Corrected course-input data ensuring constant funding stream in order to provide critical support to the forces before deployment.

ADVISOR TO LEADERSHIP: Use technical expertise in strategic planning and make recommendations to management on policies, procedures, guidelines, and processes requiring improvement, particularly related to operations and projects with special emphasis on cost efficiency and performance. Frequently briefed senior leaders at the GO/SES levels on various OCS topics and assignments.

+++ Served as the lead for coordinating GFP Tiger Team meeting involving several commands and agencies to ensure the Army is NDAA compliant by bringing all GFP to record by FY 17 while meeting all accountability and auditability standards.

+++ As Executive Officer to the Director: Designed and maintained spreadsheets that indicated division staffing allocations and on-board strength for a given time period for management use in making decisions on matters such as resource requests, recruitment priorities, distribution of resources within the division, and ratios of contractor-to-federal positions.

EFFECTIVELY COMMUNICATE AND COORDINATE WITH OTHERS: Prepare briefings, Information Papers, After Action Reports, Standard Operating Procedures (SOPs), FRAGOs, EXSUMS, and related documents to include analyzing, organizing, formatting, and ensuring accuracy/completeness of final publications. Formulate conclusions and recommendations for actions and incorporate them into formal written reports and oral presentations for various levels of management and senior leaders. Establish liaison with command organizations, higher headquarters, and other agencies to ensure maximum effort is applied to attain and sustain logistic operations.

+++ Developed and compiled briefs tracking all Army retrograde equipment out of Afghanistan for senior leaders.

+++ Coordinate with Army Service Component Commands, Combatant Commands, the Joint Chiefs of Staff, and other Army Agencies to ensure the most current and accurate information and to provide timely responses to transportation and sustainment challenges. Provided retrograde updates for General Officer Steering Committees and Council of Colonels.

MM/YYYY–MM/YYYY, POSITION TITLE, Company, Hours/week: 40, Salary: $XX, Supervisor: Name, Phone

PROVIDED EXPERT PROGRAM MANAGEMENT: Planned and formulated program execution of varied and complex supply management elements. Regularly maintained knowledge of applicable laws, regulations, and policies to ensure compliance. Analyzed interrelated issues of effectiveness, efficiency, and productivity of substantive mission-oriented programs and developed criteria for evaluating program effectiveness. Evaluated needs and developed, planned, executed, and managed communication strategies. Identified key priorities and tactical steps in order to meet deadlines associated with multiple concurrent projects.

LOGISTICS, EQUIPMENT, AND PROPERTY MANAGEMENT: Oversaw provision and logistical support of secondary items for FireFinder, a counter-mortar radar-weapon system. Supplied expendable property and equipment, controlled expendable items, and fixed assets to meet fielded demands from the Warfighter. Prepared and coordinated receipt, disposition, and distribution/redistribution of supplies and equipment. Provided technical guidance, advice, and solutions for any unusual supply problem. Maintained inventory and administered supply support to units requisitioning FireFinder secondary items. Managed, planned, and scheduled the acquisition of secondary supply items to coincide with demand planning and production lead times.

BUDGET/FINANCE: Participated in the development of project budgets and managed budget execution. Completed demand planning, budget stratifications, requisition processing, funding requests, procurement work directives, and management of assigned FireFinder secondary items.

MM/YYYY–MM/YYYY, POSITION TITLE, Company, Hours/week: 40, Salary: $XX, Supervisor: Name, Phone

SECRET SECURITY CLEARANCE

PROJECT LEADER AND TEAM MEMBER: Worked as a member of an interdisciplinary team and participated in the development of valid and effective evaluation findings, analyses, and study recommendations. Professionally interacted with staff and lead meetings and work groups. Expressed thoughts and opinions in a logical sequence as a team member and interpreted and communicated facts as part of planning and implementing the project.

+++ Completed Master of Business Administration at Texas A&M—Texarkana and graduated with a 4.0 GPA.

+++ Completed ALLC curriculum at Red River Army Depot, Texas, and graduated with honors.

MM/YYYY–MM/YYYY, POSITION TITLE, Company, Hours/week: 40, Salary: $XX, Supervisor: Name, Phone

PROGRAM ANALYST: Reviewed organizational structure, work methods, and procedures, and recommended improvements and simplifications. Performed research and evaluation for studies, reports, impact statements, and publications. Evaluated maintenance programs, reviewed performance data, and reported statistical information, uncovering logistical problem areas to determine root causes. Monitored progress toward meeting the logistics plan and identified cause and impact of delays and other problems. Adjusted plans and schedule for all related actions as required by delays and changes to logistics requirements. Evaluated plans for and provision of logistical support for feasibility, efficiency, and economy, and developed alternatives.

EXPERT STRATEGIC PLANNING: Applied analytic, diagnostic, and qualitative techniques to effectively identify, evaluate, and recommend appropriate solutions to resolve complex, interrelated issues. Interpreted information and facilitated decisions that impacted strategy, policy, and plans. Possessed understanding of the strategic and operational level policies of the military, including those with global significance.

PROJECT MANAGER AND TEAM LEADER: Improved process efficiencies as team lead in the Continuous Process Improvement branch. Directed, planned, and conducted studies for efficiency of operations within the command. Served as project manager of ad hoc teams and committees to implement special projects for the Command to include preliminary research and fact-finding, gathering, and compiling pertinent data, developing plans, surveys, spreadsheets, reports, and briefings for the Lean Six Sigma (LSS) Deployment Director. Expert skill in leading people by providing guidance, training, and coaching on organizational effectiveness and efficiency and business development to management and operational personnel.

PERFORMED ONGOING QUALITATIVE AND QUANTITATIVE ANALYSIS to measure program performance and efficiency. Analyzed data to evaluate techniques, approaches, trends, and future requirements. Analyzed functions and workloads to determine staffing requirements. Used established statistical techniques, reliability modeling, and quantitative and qualitative analysis to improve inefficient processes. Evaluated the efficiency of the command's organizational structure, staffing, and work processes and formulated recommendations for improvement.

+++ Updated office metrics for command reporting and tracked the progress of several ACC stationing plans; discovered that stationing plans were needed during the standup of ACC across the continental US and overseas.

USED COMPUTER APPLICATIONS, such as database management, word processing, and presentation software, to produce a wide variety of materials to include, but not limited to, briefings, spreadsheets, strategic plans, procedures, memoranda, correspondence, and presentations. Created flowcharts and graphics to convey complex information in easily understood format to audiences with varying levels of understanding of the topic.

BUILDING COALITIONS: Effectively collaborated with interagency partners by focusing on improving coordinated state and federal responses for domestic contingency operations. Performed liaison between staff and supported personnel to improve the effectiveness of support activities, conducted inspections, and provided technical assistance to commanders.

MM/YYYY–MM/YYYY, POSITION TITLE, Company, Hours/week: 40, Salary: $XX, Supervisor: Name, Phone

PROVIDED TECHNICAL AND OPERATIONAL SUPPORT to the personnel security program. Screened incoming military clearance records for accuracy and completeness and updated the Command personnel security database. Served as a Security Assistant and primary point of contact on various security issues, policies, and procedures related to the command. Managed the receipt, processing, issuing, and destruction of COMSEC materials and equipment in accordance with army regulations in support of command BRAC to Scott Air Force Base, Illinois.

+++ Successful transition of the Command during the Base Realignment and Closure (BRAC) move from Alexandria, VA, to Scott Air Force Base, IL.

INTERPRETED REGULATIONS: Enforced federal, state, and local laws, rules, and regulations. Maintained sensitive informational databases used for all new employees and contractors. Evaluated program operations to ensure compliance with program regulations and requirements. Ensured consistency and adherence to laws, policies, mission, and requirements.

MM/YYYY–MM/YYYY, POSITION TITLE, Company, Hours/week: 40, Salary: $XX, Supervisor: Name, Phone

PUBLIC AFFAIRS AND ADMINISTRATIVE SUPPORT: Developed plans for official functions and coordinated facilitates and personnel needed for events and symposiums. Attended and assisted in the coordination and planning of job fairs, yearly training symposiums, VIP visits, retirements, and award ceremonies. Received and conducted analysis of staff actions received from higher headquarters.

EDUCATION

Master in Business Administration, University, City, State, Zip

Bachelor of Science, University, City, State, Zip

JOB-RELATED TRAINING

+ Graduated Army Materiel Command (AMC) Fellows Program (2013)

+ DAWIA Level III certified in Life Cycle Logistics (2013)

+ US Army Lean Six Sigma Black Belt Certified (2009)

+ Completed Contracting Officer Representative (COR) Comprehension Training (2013)

+ Completed the following Civilian Education System (CES) courses:

+ Army Management Staff College Intermediate Course (2012)

+ Army Management Staff College Basic Course (2011)

+ Manager Development Course (2011)

+ Supervisor Development Course (2011)

+ Army Foundation Course (2010)

PROFESSOR

Name

Address

Phone

E-mail

MM/YYYY–Present, PROFESSIONAL PROFILE, Career Summary, Hours/week: 40

PROGRAM SPECIALIST with more than 20 years of management expertise in various business settings. Demonstrated expertise in project management, data analysis, information management, and improving operations. Proven analytical skills with the ability to investigate and evaluate facts and draw appropriate conclusions. Gifted communicator with dynamic interpersonal, oral, and written communication skills. Outstanding ability to establish priorities, multitask, and meet strict deadlines. Team player with strong organizational, research, and management skills and abilities. Proven proficiency in developing innovative solutions to problems and achieving results. Ability to handle confidential correspondence with the highest level of confidentially, prioritize tasks, meet time-sensitive deadlines, and work independently or with a team to achieve goals.

CLEARANCE: Understand the SF-86 and security clearance process; prepared to complete.

AREAS OF EXPERTISE: Program management and evaluation; project lifecycle management; program training; clinical documentation review; strategic planning; trial safety/efficacy; statistical analysis; administrative management; process improvement and simplification; team and project leadership; data entry; data collection/evaluation; evidence reviewing; document management; accurate reporting; patient care; time management; team leadership; study protocols; database coordination; technical, regulatory, and best-practices research; policy analysis; and excellent oral and written communication skills.

TECHNICAL/COMPUTER SKILLS: Microsoft Office Suite (Word, Excel, Access, PowerPoint, Outlook); Adobe; and ability to conduct credible research using the Internet.

ENDORSEMENTS:

TO BE LISTED HERE: A FEW SENTENCES ABOUT HOW GREAT YOU ARE FROM LINKEDIN, PERFORMANCE EVALUATIONS, AND LETTERS OF RECOMMENDATION.

MM/YYYY–MM/YYYY, POSITION TITLE, Company, Hours/week: 40, Salary: $XX, Supervisor: Name, Phone

EXPERT PROGRAM MANAGEMENT: Established long-range, intermediate-range, and short-range plans. Allocated and identified resources and provided a reporting and evaluation system to determine program effectiveness. Keen professional knowledge of program concepts, principles, practices, and procedures. Ensured thorough collection and input of student data for program evaluation to measure progress.

+++ Leveraged strong communications and liaison skills to establish a high level of trust with students. Quickly mastered the political environment and became adept in discerning with whom and when to share sensitive and confidential information.

ASSESSED OPERATIONAL PRODUCTIVITY, EFFECTIVENESS, AND EFFICIENCY OF PROGRAM AND PROJECTS. Provided complex quantitative and qualitative analysis to measure project effectiveness and efficiency. Sought root causes of problems with organizational policies and processes and worked to resolve them. Synthesized data into succinct reports to demonstrate needs to adjust policies and procedures. Provided risk analysis to determine potential courses of action. Implemented change management strategies in areas of delegated responsibility.

ESTABLISHED INSTRUCTIONAL DESIGN: Taught and coordinated classroom activities, such as preparing lesson plans and coordinating external program projects. Proactively led sessions to improve student understanding of the key topics and objectives in the course. Developed coursework and syllabi for classrooms. Effectively worked with faculty members to carry out assigned programs. Used knowledge of educational concepts to write lesson plans and plan workshops.

MEASURED STUDENT PERFORMANCE THROUGH VARIOUS EVALUATING METHODS, ensuring performance requirements, program policies, learning objectives, and goals were accurately followed. Used problem-resolution skills to adapt to ever-changing educational environment. Worked with students to achieve high success rates as measured by pass rates on assessments and successful completion of the course.

COUNSELED AND MENTORED STUDENTS in the topics needed to successfully complete the assessments in the course and provide feedback on assignments as appropriate. Mentored students in effective study practices relevant to the discipline(s) covered in the course and assisted students. Discussed and probed at-risk students about the problems they were facing regarding the subject and helped them overcome those challenges. Engaged students in supplemental activities that reinforced course concepts and built student confidence. Used available teaching aids such as charts and PowerPoint presentations to convey the subject matter to students. Enhanced overall class interaction.

EFFECTIVE COMMUNICATOR: Possessed strong, effective communication skills that were required in ever-changing, demanding environments. Well-versed in various methods of communicating information, lesson plans, assignments, and expectations to students. Presented novel subject matter with nontraditional instructional tools. Consistently strived to create a learning environment for students to ask questions, request assistance, and get help.

BUILT AND MAINTAINED EFFECTIVE WORKING RELATIONSHIPS: Collaborated with others to generate ideas and lesson plans based on program goals. Facilitated a positive working process by setting high standards for collaboration among the students. Encouraged program students to explore their creative interests and produce projects.

MM/YYYY–MM/YYYY, POSITION TITLE, Company, Hours/week: 40, Salary: $XX, Supervisor: Name, Phone

SERVED AS COLLEGE INSTRUCTOR for Introduction to Psychology program students in a nationally accredited institution of higher education. The class was an introduction to the problems, methods and concepts of psychology, covering a range of topics that characterize the discipline, including history; methodology and professional ethics; biological foundations; perception; motivation and emotion; learning; memory and thinking; individual differences; intelligence; personality; behavior disorders and their treatment; and group processes. Developed and used informal and formal techniques and instruments to facilitate a high-quality learning experience. Reviewed and modified teaching strategies when needed. Infused existing course curriculum with new ideas and examples. Created group exercise experiences and introduced students to the steps in conducting research and a library experience to reinforce concepts.

TAUGHT ORAL AND WRITTEN COMMUNICATION SKILLS offered within the program of study. Managed student results through creating and maintaining conducive learning environments, preparing effective classroom lessons and lectures, administering effective teaching and coaching techniques, performing student evaluations toward meeting course objectives, and mentoring students needing assistance. Used full range of Microsoft Office programs extensively. Developed syllabi and created tests to assess students in the following areas: Knowledge, Comprehension, Application, Analysis, Synthesis, and Evaluation.

EDUCATION

Degree, Concentration, University, City, State, Zip

Name

Phone

E-mail

Address

Work Experience

01/2008—Present, PROFESSIONAL PROFILE, Career Summary, Home Address, Hours/week: 40

TOP SECRET/SENSITIVE COMPARTMENTED INFORMATION (TS/SCI) WITH CI POLY

PROFESSIONAL PROFILE: LAW ENFORCEMENT PROFESSIONAL with more than 5 years of progressive experience providing analysis and strategic planning. Very strong critical-thinking, problem-solving, research, and liaison skills. Recognized for outstanding communication skills, flexibility, keen political savvy, sense of humor, and leadership abilities.

AREAS OF EXPERTISE: Program evaluation and management; strategic and operations planning; workforce analysis and planning; security oversight; process improvement and simplification; team and project leadership; quantitative/qualitative analysis; risk and feasibility assessment; technical, regulatory, and best-practices research; policy analysis; negotiating; and oral and written communication skills.

TECHNICAL SKILLS: Microsoft Office Suite (Word, Excel, Outlook, PowerPoint); and expert ability to conduct credible Internet-based research.

ENDORSEMENTS:

TO BE LISTED HERE: A FEW SENTENCES ABOUT HOW GREAT YOU ARE FROM LINKEDIN, PERFORMANCE EVALUATIONS, AND LETTERS OF RECOMMENDATION.

MM/YYYY–MM/YYYY, POSITION TITLE, Company, Hours/week: 40, Salary: $XX, Supervisor: Name, Phone

SERVE AS AN ENFORCEMENT OFFICER deterring and detecting violations by conducting visible, uniformed patrols and inspections. Conduct arrests, searches, and seizures in accordance with the US Constitution, pertinent laws, regulations, directives, and court decisions. Conduct administrative investigations, review case reports, and arrest documents. Conduct investigations of law violations, interview victims, and preserve and protect areas to be investigated. Plan strategies for investigations as required, including scheduling, developing plan of action, following up, and closing out of investigations. Apply reasonable judgment using these regulations to solve public problems and apprehend criminals. Extensive experience in multidiscipline intelligence and counterintelligence operations, law enforcement, and national security investigations.

APPLY EXCEPTIONAL INVESTIGATIVE/INSPECTOR TECHNIQUES: Organize and schedule ongoing investigative activities and revise plans and assignments as unexpected problems requiring new lines of inquiry evolve. Use rapport building, active listening, body language, written statement analysis, and interview techniques to conduct interviews and interrogations for criminal investigations. Employ various methods of investigation to understand personal, financial, and community criminal issues. Successful in developing investigative leads and obtaining confessions from criminal suspects. Compile reports from various law enforcement agencies for use in investigations. Review summaries of information pertaining to subjects under investigation. Use Threat Management strategies and mitigation techniques used by the US Marshals Service.

TECHNICAL EXPERTISE: UNDERSTAND LEGAL MATTERS and use knowledge to interpret regulations such as the Code of Federal Regulations, US Code, and the laws, rules, and regulations of the US government. Interpret and apply expert knowledge to investigations and public safety work. Review cases for consistency and compliance with established rules and regulations for criminal procedure. Establish and maintain warrant files/warrant working files in accordance with regulations and policies. Comply with all existing policies, procedures, and guidelines (including the use of force policy) pertaining to use, display, safety, and maintenance of firearms and intermediate weapons. Enforce federal laws and ensure DOD and NGA rules and regulations are followed.

+++ Respect rights of persons involved in incidents such as right to privacy (Privacy Act Amendment of 1974), civil rights, right to be treated fairly and impartially, and the Freedom of Information Act. Explain confidentiality issues to sources and take sworn statements. Secure sensitive information appropriately.

MAINTAIN HIGH LEVEL OF AWARENESS on matters of safety and security and understand different levels of risk and threat, paying utmost attention to detail. Ability to think and act quickly in rapidly changing environments, using judgment to identify threats against facilities and employees. Routinely work under difficult conditions and under high levels of stress.

DATA GATHERING AND REPORTING: Document all apparent violations of NGA statutes detected during the course of patrols and inspections. Collect, identify, and preserve evidence (including witness statements) associated with any violation and assemble a complete case report. Prepare accident, incident, and security violation reports. Prepare case files and reports for submission/ adjudication and monitor progress.

EXPERT SKILL IN USING VARIOUS SOFTWARE PACKAGES/DATABASES: Access, update, maintain, verify, and extract from an information database. Use Microsoft Word to prepare reports and other documents. Access and update information using National Crime Information Center system. Access and update information using any other public database. Perform computerized research using law enforcement database systems. Input, review, and maintenance of data in law enforcement databases.

EFFECTIVELY COMMUNICATE, LIAISE, AND BUILD AND MAINTAIN WORKING RELATIONSHIPS: Engage in effective, proactive oral and written communication, often under difficult and highly emotional circumstances, with widely diverse individuals. Develop questions; interview prospective employees and other parties. Draft numerous reports, compose and secure court orders, subpoenas, and search warrants. Testify in state and federal courts. Conduct follow-up when necessary and appropriate.

MM/YYYY–MM/YYYY, POSITION TITLE, Company, Hours/week: 40, Salary: $XX, Supervisor: Name, Phone

PROPERTY AND PERSONNEL SECURITY: Escorted uncleared personnel in and out of secured areas. Ensured the area requiring access was properly sanitized and prepared for uncleared personnel to enter. Assisted DIA police in case of emergency events. Relocated Mobile Disaster Control equipment to a designated location outside of the facilities. Verified visitors entering the agency were in the security database and had the proper clearance to access the SCIF or other secured area. Independently followed guidelines, demonstrated resilience, and planned, evaluated, and solved problems, multitasking effectively and efficiently. Provided expert customer service, teamwork, interpersonal, and conflict-management skills.

+++ Demonstrated high degree of professionalism, advanced organizational abilities, communication, and diplomacy skills. Successful in assisting senior-level management execute the strategic vision by providing expert support, advice, and consultation on programs and operations.

PROVIDED EXCELLENT CUSTOMER SERVICE through analysis of customer feedback and focus of attention on areas requiring improvement. Engaged and interacted with the public, giving directions and responding to inquiries. Identified and fulfilled public needs with services within sphere of influence. Dealt with challenging client issues, resolving them by implementing win-win solutions. Recognized by management for exceptional customer service practices.

MANAGED AND MANIPULATED COMPUTER SOFTWARE PROGRAMS, including developing and maintaining Excel spreadsheets. Utilized professional computer knowledge, skills, and abilities to operate the following software systems and programs: Microsoft Office Suite, including MS Word, Excel, and PowerPoint.

DEVELOPED AND MAINTAINED PROFESSIONAL RELATIONSHIPS: Conducted cooperative investigative tasks associated with cases assigned to other entities and solicited support for assigned cases outside of local jurisdiction. Promoted team approach to work and share/seek information from internal and external sources.

MM/YYYY–MM/YYYY, POSITION TITLE, Company, Hours/week: 40, Salary: $XX, Supervisor: Name, Phone

SECURITY PROGRAM SPECIALIST: Supported Security Education and Awareness program by developing and presenting a wide range of security-related briefings. Managed the PD security access program involving processes and procedures for obtaining access to security programs. Oversaw issuance and control of DOD, DIA, and Intelligence Community (IC) identification cards and security/access control badges, including DIA security badges, IC badges, courier badges, and Common Access Cards (CAC). Maintained an accurate inventory by ordering badge stock, forms, and supplies. Independently performed a wide variety of functions for the FD Security Division involving multiple security disciplines.

CONDENSED ANALYZED INFORMATION AND DATA INTO AN ABBREVIATED FORMAT for management. Collected and analyzed data to prepare investigative reports. Ensured reports revealed clear, concise summarization of information while precisely representing numerous pages of case notes. Effectively conveyed technical information. Gathered, tracked, and reported designated actions resulting from project status meetings. Compiled and distributed Branch Reports, using the DIA Central Tasking System.

STRATEGIC PLANNING: INTERPRETED FACTS AND ANALYZED COMPLEX SITUATIONS related to strategic engagements. Applied analytic, diagnostic, and qualitative techniques to effectively identify, evaluate, and recommend appropriate solutions to resolve complex issues.

EXPERT ORAL AND WRITTEN COMMUNICATION AND INTERPERSONAL SKILLS: Served as liaison for sensitive compartmented information and special access programs. Provided technical advice and recommendations in the form of oral and written briefings, reports, and presentations to senior leadership. Presented analysis findings to management through oral briefings and the preparation of periodic written reports. Leveraged strong communication and liaison skills to establish a high level of trust with senior staff. Conducted Sensitive Compartmented Information (SCI) indoctrinations/briefings.

MM/YYYY–MM/YYYY, POSITION TITLE, Company, Hours/week: 40, Salary: $XX, Supervisor: Name, Phone

INFORMATION GATHERING AND SECURITY: Protected all Sensitive Compartmented Information utilized by Department of State policy decision makers within four strategic goals of Department of State. Verified and signed the badge requests form DS-1838. Ensured that SCI debriefings were entered immediately upon notification. Prepared and provided briefings and debriefing for Special Access Programs materials as required. Received controlled and safeguarded Secured Compartmented Information and National Classified material. Prepared SCI and collateral materials for shipment to other agency sites in accordance with applicable security-handling procedures.

FIRST RESPONDER: Responded to emergency and nonemergency incidents including accidents, fire, disturbances, and other misdemeanor and felony crimes. Provided first aid to injured persons and authored incident and accident reports involving stolen property and criminal activities. Operated equipment including firearms and special weapons.

MM/YYYY–MM/YYYY, POSITION TITLE, Company, Hours/week: 40, Salary: $XX, Supervisor: Name, Phone

NATIONAL PARK PROTECTION AND SECURITY: Verified that visitors entering the agency were in the security database and had the proper clearance to access the SCIF. Ability to enforce fish and wildlife laws. Studied, observed, and wrote about local, state, and federal statutes and regulations for the conservation and management of natural resources.

SUPERVISED AND MANAGED more than 60 personnel. Keen ability to coordinate complex tasks and teams, including partnerships with other entities. Oversaw performance management for each employee: development and evaluation of performance plans, mentoring, and coaching for Individual Development Plans, and performance counseling and coaching. Took disciplinary action when necessary to ensure acceptable conduct and completion of operations according to established procedures.

CONTRACT OVERSIGHT: Oversaw the operation of the security contract valued in excess of $1 million. Performed qualitative and quantitative analysis to measure contract performance and efficiency. Analyzed data to evaluate techniques, approaches, trends, and future requirements.

MM/YYYY–MM/YYYY, POSITION TITLE, Company, Hours/week: 40, Salary: $XX, Supervisor: Name, Phone

PROVIDED FULL RANGE OF PHYSICAL SECURITY SERVICES to protect life and property. Prevented, deterred, denied, and detected investigating criminal acts, and mitigated deadly behavior. Monitored counterintelligence principles and took part in recurring training to ensure mission readiness in regard to these principles. Used knowledge of military techniques and strategic planning skills to provide advice and support. Executed raid missions, foot patrols, security checkpoints, boat patrols, personal protection missions, guard duties, convoy security, reconnaissance operations, and static and mobile security operations.

JOB-RELATED TRAINING

State Department (Document Security Branch Control Officer) required training

Federal Law Enforcement Training Center, UPTP

+ Certified SAP and SSRP Control Officer

+ First Aid—CPR AED, Adult, Child, and Infant

+ MEB Baton Certification

+ ASE Certified X-Ray Machine Technician

ADDITIONAL INFORMATION

VOLUNTEER EXPERIENCE

YYYY–YYYY, Commission Youth Counselor

Name

Phone

Address

E-mail

MM/YYYY–Present, PROFESSIONAL PROFILE, Career Summary, Hours/week: 40

PROGRAM MANAGER/ANALYST with more than 15 years of progressive experience providing analysis, strategic planning, program, and project management. Expertise in strategic and tactical planning, program and management analysis, and resource analysis and optimization. Solid record of performance managing analytical studies, key initiatives, and high-profile performance-improvement projects. Technical expert and analyst on complex program issues. Very strong critical-thinking, problem-solving, research, and liaison skills. Recognized for outstanding communication skills, flexibility, keen political savvy, sense of humor, and leadership abilities.

CLEARANCE: Understand the SF-86 and security clearance process; prepared to complete.

AREAS OF EXPERTISE: Program evaluation and management; project lifecycle management; strategic and operations planning; human resources management; workforce analysis and planning; operational, compliance auditing; internal control reviews; process improvement and simplification; team and project leadership; quantitative/qualitative analysis; risk and feasibility assessment; technical, regulatory, and best-practices research; policy analysis; negotiating; social marketing; and excellent oral and written communication skills.

ENDORSEMENTS:

TO BE LISTED HERE: A FEW SENTENCES ABOUT HOW GREAT YOU ARE FROM LINKEDIN, PERFORMANCE EVALUATIONS, AND LETTERS OF RECOMMENDATION.

MM/YYYY–MM/YYYY, POSITION TITLE, Company, Hours/week: 40, Salary: $XX, Supervisor: Name, Phone

EXPERT PROGRAM AND PROJECT MANAGER: Maintain operational productivity, effectiveness, and efficiency of the Mid-Atlantic Program, which includes federal, state, and commercial accounts in Southern California. Evaluate client public affairs and community outreach needs, and develop, plan, execute, and manage communication strategies that ensure consistency and adherence to laws, policies, mission, and requirements. Identify key priorities and tactical steps in order to meet deadlines associated with multiple concurrent projects. Consistently exceed performance goals through development of innovative action plans, project management, and stakeholder outreach.

+++ Demonstrate high degree of professionalism, advanced organizational abilities, communication, and diplomacy skills. Successful in assisting senior-level management execute the strategic vision by providing expert support, advice, and consultation on program management and analysis, project management, and strategic financial programs and operations.

ASSESS OPERATIONAL PRODUCTIVITY, EFFECTIVENESS, AND EFFICIENCY OF PROGRAM AND PROJECTS. Provide complex quantitative and qualitative analysis to measure project effectiveness and efficiency. Seek root causes of problems with organizational policies and processes and work to resolve them. Analyze data to determine compliance with established regulations and organizational policies, management principles, rules, and guidelines. Synthesize data into succinct reports to demonstrate needs to adjust policies and procedures. Provide risk analysis to determine potential courses of action. Implement change-management strategies in areas of delegated responsibility. Train and supervise others in methods for analyzing and organizing data and reports.

ADVISE MANAGEMENT on current industry trends, technologies, and best management practices. Research, study, and analyze policies, laws, and regulations of various federal, state, and commercial programs and make recommendations to senior management on how to adjust policies accordingly. Use technical expertise in strategic planning and make recommendations to management on policies, procedures, guidelines, and processes requiring improvement, particularly related to operations and projects with special emphasis on cost efficiency and performance.

ENSURE PERFORMANCE METRICS AND MEASURES are achieved, often exceeding desired levels. Provide expert oversight for the successful completion of projects and analyze metrics to track performance. Monitor results versus targets and provide gap-analysis to achieve strategic goals and performance objectives. Consistently meet or exceed management and organizational strategic goals and objectives through implementation of short-term and long-term projects and action plans.

FINANCE/ BUDGET: Analyze need for human resource capital and various operations related to contract fulfillment and make recommendations to senior management on resource allocation. Provide revenue projections using Excel. Adhere to budget guidelines for program expenses. Provide detailed monthly expense reports.

DIRECT SUPERVISOR of 10 staff. Keen ability to coordinate complex tasks and teams, including partnerships with other entities. Oversee performance management for each employee: development and evaluation of performance plans, mentoring and coaching for Individual Development Plans, and performance counseling and coaching. Take disciplinary action when necessary to ensure acceptable conduct and completion of operations according to established procedures.

USE COMPUTER APPLICATIONS such as MS Excel, Word, and PowerPoint to produce a wide variety of materials to include, but not limited to, briefings, spreadsheets, strategic plans, procedures, memoranda, correspondence, and presentations. Create flowcharts and graphics to convey complex information in easily understood format to audiences with varying levels of understanding of the topic.

EXPERT ORAL AND WRITTEN COMMUNICATION SKILLS: Conduct meetings and provide presentations to groups and individual key stakeholders using appropriate software and superior communication skills. Write, edit, and present status reports, working papers, briefings, strategic plans, and proposals. Generate clear and succinct daily, weekly, monthly, and quarterly financial and forecasting reports. Write and edit presentations and train management and employees on operational procedures and best practices.

TEAM LEADER: Directly lead a cross-functional group of three team members collaborating regularly with Business Development Specialist and Account Manager to develop business strategies to meet measurable performance benchmarks. Expert skill in leading people by providing guidance, training, and coaching on organizational effectiveness and efficiency and business development to management and operational personnel.

PROVIDE EXCELLENT CUSTOMER SERVICE through analysis of customer feedback and focus of attention on areas requiring improvement. Identify and fulfill client needs with products and services within sphere of influence. Recognized by management and clients for exceptional customer service practices.

BUILD AND MAINTAIN EFFECTIVE WORKING RELATIONSHIPS in a team environment. Educate, advise, negotiate, collaborate, and build support for ideas and initiatives, tactfully and diplomatically addressing issues that are in contention or sensitive. Serve as expert liaison between government entities and company and establish high level of trust with and between corporate staff and clients. Provide professional assistance to coworkers and other staff on operational issues of projects.

MM/YYYY–MM/YYYY, POSITION TITLE, Company, Hours/week: 40, Salary: $XX, Supervisor: Name, Phone

EXPERT PROGRAM MANAGER with excellent business acumen in the areas of finance, resource allocation, and leveraging of technical resources. Provided exceptional client service by assessing client needs, maintaining high-quality standards, and evaluating client satisfaction. Dealt with challenging client issues, resolving them by implementing win-win solutions. Program operations spanned throughout Maryland, Virginia, West Virginia, and the District of Columbia.

PROGRAM EVALUATION: CONDUCTED FREQUENT REVIEWS to keep process on track, gauge progress, and assess milestones and technical requirement deadlines. Coordinated resources for participation in performance benchmarking of complex contracts.

PERFORMED ONGOING QUALITATIVE AND QUANTITATIVE ANALYSIS to measure contract and program performance and efficiency. Analyzed data to evaluate techniques, approaches, trends, and future requirements. Analyzed functions and workloads to determine staffing requirements. Developed new plans, schedules, and methods to accommodate changing requirements.

CONTRACT MANAGER: Evaluated, negotiated, planned, administered, and managed federal, state, and local government and nongovernmental contracts for published educational materials and services. Identified key priorities and tactical steps and met deadlines associated with concurrent projects while generating profitable business growth.

NEGOTIATING SKILLS: Used expert negotiation and consensus-building skills to ensure award of complicated contracts. Negotiated pricing, time frames, terms, and product specifications during precontract phase. Negotiated change orders, modifications, contract terminations, and contract renewals. Analyzed, organized, and presented data in a convincing manner to support negotiations with clients.

ADVISED MANAGEMENT: Interacted with management to review and develop strategic goals. Made recommendations to senior-level management regarding organizational goals, plans, and policies to successfully develop and maintain effective relations with customers and clients.

HIGHLY EFFECTIVE ORAL AND WRITTEN COMMUNICATION SKILLS: Effectively used e-mail, written correspondence, and presentations to convey key information, summarize decisions, and explain procedures. Condensed technical data and financial information into succinct and organized pieces for incorporation into easily understood reports and presentations.

Name

Address

Phone

E-mail

Work Experience

MM/YYYY–Present, PROFESSIONAL PROFILE, Career Summary, Hours/week: 40

BUSINESS PROFESSIONAL with education and progressive experience in analysis and international relations. Solid record of performance. Very strong critical-thinking, problem-solving, research, and liaison skills. Studying and learning a proficiency in Spanish. Recognized for outstanding communication skills, flexibility, keen political savvy, sense of humor, and leadership abilities.

CLEARANCE: Understand the SF-86 and security clearance process; prepared to complete.

AREAS OF EXPERTISE: International relations; public policy; intelligence; terrorism; policy analysis; process improvement and simplification; team and project leadership; quantitative/qualitative analysis; technical, regulatory, and best-practices research; and excellent oral and written communication skills.

TECHNICAL SKILLS: Microsoft Office Suite (Word, Excel, Outlook, and PowerPoint); Lotus Notes; able to conduct credible and Internet-based research.

ENDORSEMENTS:

TO BE LISTED HERE: A FEW SENTENCES ABOUT HOW GREAT YOU ARE FROM LINKEDIN, PERFORMANCE EVALUATIONS, AND LETTERS OF RECOMMENDATION.

MM/YYYY–Present, TEAM LEADER AND TEAM MEMBER, University, Address, Hours/week: 40 Salary: $0000, Academic Advisor: Name, Phone

BACHELOR OF SCIENCE in INTERNATIONAL RELATIONS, STRATEGIC INTELLIGENCE

RELEVANT COURSEWORK: International Relations; Political Economy Public Policy; Introduction to Intelligence; History of Intelligence; Terrorism; Military Intelligence; Strategic Intelligence; Constitutional History; Political Theory; Introduction to Intelligence Analysis.

PROJECT COORDINATION SKILLS: Review project requirements on International Relations to effectively delegate tasks and establish time lines. Demonstrate skill in defining project scope and details. Create project plans on foreign relations and military intelligence by identifying tasks to be performed, necessary requirements, deliverables, and milestones. Recommend and devise individual scopes of work. Manage data and information collection and research. Monitor results in alignment with project goals and objectives. Actively encourage communication, coordination, innovation, and high-quality team products.

INDEPENDENTLY RESEARCH AND ANALYZE highly complex policy, strategy, and conceptual issues involving current and past policies dealing with public policy. Compile and analyze data to develop comprehensive research reports on the Political Economy of International Relations (IR). Summarize findings into concise briefings.

DEMONSTRATE EFFECTIVE COMMUNICATION: Prepare a wide variety of communications, both orally and in writing, to a wide variety of audiences on complex international affairs subject matters, conveying information in plain language using graphical aids to ensure common understanding. Prepare recommendations and presentations to support policy and project decisions. Review and synthesize policy papers, reports, and white papers from various sources covering an array of International Relations topics in various geographic regions.

DEVELOP AND MAINTAIN EFFECTIVE RELATIONSHIPS: Assist in conducting meetings with relevant team members, professors, and other industry professionals. Lead teams for various projects using expert leadership and communication skills.

MM/YYYY–MM/YYYY, OFF-HOURS STOCK CREW, Toys R US, Hours/week: 40, Salary: $XX, Supervisor: Name, Phone

MERCHANDISE MANAGEMENT: Studied floor plans and layouts to determine best method of displaying products. Restocked merchandise, paying special interest to customer needs, marketability, and company promotion. Reviewed stock levels and gathered inventory data. Physically removed goods from a truck and placed in empty pallets, security cages, and transferred back on the truck. Implemented merchandising and visual standards in department stores to leverage in-store display and marketing space based on the company policies.

MM/YYYY–MM/YYYY, CAMP COUNSELOR, Company, Hours/week: 40, Salary: $XX, Supervisor: Name, Phone

ACTIVITY COORDINATOR for three summers. Served as a role model for children and planned and organized daily and weekly camper activities. Facilitated, supervised, and participated in all games and programs with day camp participants. Provided constant and continuous supervision of all day campers while assisting with the development and administering of lesson plans for the activities. Additionally, demonstrated understanding of campers with varying capabilities, interests, and problems.

+++ Maintained required CPR and First Aid certification.

ADVISOR ON CONFIDENTIAL MATTERS: When necessary, discussed camper's sensitive issues with senior-level counselors and parents. Developed and reviewed plans for resolving issues and followed up accordingly. Appropriately handled sensitive and confidential matters with discretion.

PROVIDED CLEAR, CONCISE WRITTEN AND ORAL COMMUNICATION: Provided written and oral communications to senior-level management and parents on a consistent basis. This entailed informing them about their child's health, eating habits, play habits, and any other notable observations. Drafted and edited documents, carefully reviewing content for accuracy and consistency.

EDUCATION

Bachelor of Science in International Relations, Strategic Intelligence, Expected graduation date 05/2013, ## credit hours completed, Liberty University, Lynchburg, VA

351.73 JAC

Jackson, Corliss.

Cracking the federal job code

DEC 2 2 2016

CPSIA information can be obtained
at www.ICGtesting.com
Printed in the USA
LVOW03s1628011216

515345LV00002B/54/P

9 781491 786987